The Republican Dilemma

Conservatism or Progressivism

Duel Personality

The Republican Dilemma

Conservatism or Progressivism

CONRAD JOYNER

THE UNIVERSITY OF ARIZONA PRESS
TUCSON   1963

To
CONRAD II
MICHAEL
MARK
. . . and Ann

PREFACE

Dwight Eisenhower's election in 1952 was widely hailed as the dawn of a political age. The dominant force of this nascent age was to be a "new" policy of government variously called "Modern Republicanism," "New Republicanism," and "Eisenhower Republicanism." At the 1956 Republican National Convention in San Francisco President Eisenhower officially proclaimed the policy of "modern Republicanism." Arthur Larson in his book, *A Republican Looks at His Party,* anticipated Eisenhower's announcement and tried to distinguish this most recent genre of Republicans from those of bygone days.

The notion that Eisenhower is the original leader of this new Republicanism has gained wide currency. It is reinforced in a negative way by those in and out of his own party who brand him a "socialist" or "a conscious agent of the Communist conspiracy." The bestowing of the leadership mantle on Eisenhower is a sweeping historical generalization oversimplifying the countless forces and circumstances which combined to bring about the changed look that a portion of the party has taken on.

The public personality of Eisenhower is a convenient political symbol but as such misses the drama and struggles which have gripped the Republican party since 1932. What is even more significant, the Eisenhower myth — which makes him the creator and inspiration for the new Republicanism — serves to obscure the policies which many of the conservative Republicans have found bitter to swallow. For instance, the Rockefeller-Nixon agreement on the contents of the Republican platform prior to the 1960 convention has been dismissed by many liberals as a mere political expedient while the conservative Republicans have ignored it. Yet, this agreement is one of the clearest examples of the change which has taken place in the Republican party during the past thirty years. The points of the Nixon-Rockefeller agreement as incorporated in the 1960 Republican platform stand in marked contrast to the pledges the Republicans made to the preceding generation.

The debates over the policy content of "modern Republicanism" resemble the dialogue between Catholic priests and Protestant ministers over the meaning of the biblical text, "Thou art Peter, and upon this rock I will build my Church." Once Eisenhower, the sparkling political personality, is placed in perspective, the substance of the new Republicanism becomes apparent. It involves some fairly simple but highly significant propositions. In domestic policies modern Republicanism boils down to Arthur Larson's concession that "good" New Deal measures are to be retained and perfected. This is coupled with a healthy respect for local self-government and private enterprise. Thus, the modern Republican accepts the fact that most of the New Deal is here to stay. In foreign affairs the most important ingredient of the new Republican approach is rejection of isolationism and facing the realities of international politics which demand widespread U.S. participation in world affairs.

Eisenhower does not deserve the credit for these innovations in the policy of the GOP majority. His nomination and the policies of his administration, especially of the first two years, are but tangible evidence of the party's changed nature. In reality, the Republican party made its first truce with the domestic policies of the New Deal at the 1940 convention. At this same time the party recognized, albeit reluctantly, the necessary and legitimate role of the U.S. in foreign affairs. They embraced these points and with them "modern Republicanism" when they selected Wendell Willkie as their standard bearer.

The Republican electoral resurgence in 1952, bringing into power a Republican who followed the line articulated by Willkie, is an excellent illustration of the process by which a minority party returns to power in the U.S. two-party system. Initially the party had to discard the outmoded tenets which they had held to in the 1920's. The party did this in 1940 when they accepted a man who approved of many government sponsored socio-economic measures and who in large part renounced the isolationism of his predecessors, leaders of the party in the era of normalcy. In fact, as far as internal affairs went, the Democrats were to be outdone at their own game. By 1940, prominent Republicans and Willkie in particular were saying that they could better administer Franklin Roosevelt's programs. This was another sign that the Republicans were making the necessary adjustments which could enable them to one day become the majority party. Yet the party did not renounce all its former appeal. It maintained a fundamental link with the past by pledging to stimulate economic expansion through private rather than governmental spending.

The acceptance of modern Republicanism is painful for many Republicans, but it is part of the process in regaining majority party status. Republicans have not been able to reclaim all the glory that was once theirs. This, in part, results from the fact that the conversion to modern Republicanism is not complete. Nostalgic and passionate references to the past keep reappearing. The conservatives do not die or even fade away. Rather, they have gained prominence and been nurtured by the handsome and articulate junior senator from Arizona, Barry Goldwater. This man and his followers will make certain that the great party battles which occurred when Willkie and Eisenhower were nominated will be re-enacted with different casts at future Republican conventions.

There are some who contend that the party members do not know what has happened to them — that they are modern Republicans. The recent recollections of Willkie's nomination and the indication by political observers (such as Kenneth Crawford of *Newsweek* and the editors of the *New Republic)* that the Republicans are looking for another "Willkie" underlie the notion that the Republicans *do not know* or have forgotten what happened in the 1940 convention. In view of revival of interest in Willkie and the past two decades of strife in the GOP over policy, there are a number of questions which Republicans and all Americans need to ask. What was the plight of the Republican party in 1940? Who was Willkie? What did he stand for? Why did the Republicans want Willkie? Do they want another "Willkie" in 1964 or at any convention in the next decade?

To answer these questions one must dip into the past in order to recapture the nature of the Republicans during the 1930's, to recount the turbulent years of the man who became their spokesman in 1940, and to take stock of the more recent state of the party. Thus, the focus of the following pages will be Willkie's nomination — how it came about and what effect it had on the Republican party. In this context it is possible to engage in the hazardous sport of gazing into the political crystal ball and forecasting the future of the Republicans, particularly what kind of man they are likely to select as their presidential candidate in 1964.

In writing this short book, it seems that I have accumulated an inordinate number of debts. Bill Carleton prodded me to think about Wendell Willkie's role in the Republican party. Both Bill Carleton and Bill Havard, Head of the Department of Government at Louisiana State University, read portions of the manuscript. Currin Shields encouraged me to complete the book. Two students, Issac Burson and Larry

Downey, assisted in the preparation of the manuscript. The Institute of Government Research at the University of Arizona provided me a research grant during the summer of 1963. Mrs. Sylvia Sloan typed the final draft, and like all good secretaries added more than her technical ability at the typewriter. Jack Cross, and Elizabeth Shaw, director and associate editor of the University of Arizona Press respectively, demonstrated all the virtues that editors are not supposed to possess.

Four politicians have contributed a great deal to my knowledge of their delicate art. The late Paul Tingle who was an active participant in Indiana politics for more than four decades gave me the opportunity to work with him before I was dry behind the ears. Governor Mark Hatfield of Oregon opened the doors of his office to me for a year. Richard Burke asked me to coordinate his campaign for Congress in 1962 and it became a labor of love. And Jack Speiden, one of the truly outstanding men of Arizona politics, has fed both my mind and body on numerous occasions.

Finally, I want to express appreciation to a very special person. I often wonder if married male authors receive as much assistance from their wives as they claim. In my case, there can be no doubt that this manuscript would never have seen the printed page if it had not been for Ann Joyner. It is for this reason that the book is not dedicated to her. She asked me to dedicate it to our three young politicians, and I promised her this would be done. One of the pages at the front of the book indicates that I am not one to go back on a promise.

Since most of the people mentioned do not know that their assistance is being acknowledged, they can hardly take any responsibility for what I have written. In fact, for one reason or another, they probably would disagree with the interpretations which are scattered throughout the book. I only hope that they do not object to these acknowledgements.

Conrad Joyner,
Tucson, Arizona
1963

CONTENTS

Thomas in the Detroit News

1943 — "You Never Can Tell"

Burck in the Chicago Sun-Times

Unseated!

McMahon in the Philadelphia Bulletin

1940 — "Convention Road"

1940 • THE REPUBLICAN TRAVAIL

In 1940, the Republican party was faced with one of its greatest problems. The party had been out of power for two presidential terms and had not organized Congress for ten years, the longest period in its history. From 1860 to 1932 the Republican party virtually dominated national and state government. In selecting candidates for the presidency it had always chosen a man who had given loyal and enduring service to the party. In 1940, this practice was to be revised. The Republicans ranged far afield and nominated Wendell Willkie.

Willkie's nomination shocked Republicans who had had difficulty accepting Herbert Hoover, despite his eight years of service in the cabinets of Harding and Coolidge. Yet, at their twenty-second convention the party of Lincoln, McKinley, and Teddy Roosevelt nominated a man who had never filled either a state or national office. And what was worse, a man whose political experience had been almost exclusively gathered in the Democratic party. In large part, this unprecedented departure from tradition can be explained in terms of the plight the Republican party had reached by 1940.

Before the Great Depression the Republicans had called themselves the only party fit to govern. The party represented itself as the guarantor of national prosperity; it was the party of business and business was the American ideal. The last successful candidate the Republicans nominated — Herbert Hoover: humanitarian, engineer, and businessman — epitomized the image which the Republicans had projected in the 1920's. Amidst one of the greatest landslides in U.S. political history, Hoover carried four southern states and all the rest of the country except Rhode Island and Massachusetts in 1928.

Despite this great popular mandate the Republicans were given a minute forewarning of things to come. For the first time since 1900 the Democrats gained a small cumulative majority of votes in the twelve largest cities. In 1924, the Republicans had carried these same cities by over a million and a quarter votes! The Republican policy of leaving social and economic policies to the local units of government was a key factor in this urban shift. This policy was unrealistic since the states, counties, and cities had done very little to relieve the social and economic plight of the cities. The Depression which began in 1929 shoved the urban voter further into the Democratic camp. Moreover, the Depression greatly affected the composition of Congress. In 1930, the Republicans lost control of the House for the first time since 1918.

As the Depression increased in severity, it produced a different picture of the business man and the Republicans who represented him. The business man was portrayed as being confused and predatory, operating only by the profit motive, a George Babbitt, an incompetent in the grip of forces that he had unleashed in a blind drive for material gain. In 1932, business and the Republican party received the full force of the Depression reaction. The Republicans nominated Hoover again, but this proved to be only a formality to keep the party in the field.

When the Republicans gathered at Cleveland in 1936 for their national convention, atavistic thoughts were the order of the day. In his keynote address, Hoover denounced the New Deal as fascist and Roosevelt as a dictator. He called for a "Holy Crusade for Freedom." The convention accepted a platform condemning the New Deal as dishonoring American traditions and pledging the GOP to "the preservation of traditional free enterprise." The foreign policy plank did little more than emulate the one of 1924 — "America shall not become a member of the League of Nations."

To carry the banner of free enterprise and isolation, the Republicans turned to a man who had never held federal office and selected Governor Alf Landon of Kansas. He was nominated on the first ballot, because he appeared to be the only acceptable candidate. Colorless though he was, Landon was one of the eight Republican governors in the U.S. He was one of the few men of national prominence in the party who had won in the face of the Democratic landslides of 1932 and 1934.

The Republican nominee of 1936 was not as hostile to the New Deal as many of his fellow Republicans. He was a middle-of-the-road candidate around whom the party could present a unified front. It was hoped that Landon as an unmagnetic, common-sense, business-like man would be a symbol around which those who were dissatisfied with the New Deal could rally. Further, Landon's nomination, since he accepted some economic and social reforms, was a recognition by the Republicans of the validity of some of the New Deal schemes. This move was in vain because the country was not yet willing to trust the party which had been in power when the Depression started. The Democratic candidates of 1936 did their best to remind the voters of this fact.

Despite the overwhelming 1936 victory the New Deal was beginning to lose some of its appeal by 1940. As a matter of fact, the last measure of the New Deal was the Wages and Hours Act of mid-1938. As the New Deal dynamo began to slow down, the Republicans began to regain strength. In the off-year election of 1938, the Republicans picked up eight additional senators and eighty-one representatives, boosting their total to twenty-seven in the Senate and 170 in the House. In 1938, the Republicans' largest gains were in the midwest where they changed a 78 to 36 minority into a 77 to 41 majority in the House of Representatives.

The 1938 Republican gains did not mean that the party was about to return to power. The Democrats still had sixty-nine senators to the Republicans' twenty-seven, and 261 representatives to the Republicans' 170. The reason why the Republicans were no nearer to returning to power was that they faced a challenge which they had not successfully met. Throughout the 1930's, President Roosevelt and the New Deal had spent taxes and borrowed money in large and growing amounts for pensions, crop subsidies, slum clearance projects, unemployment relief, and cheap power projects. On the strength of support gained for these measures, the New Deal effected a farmer-labor political base, such as had been in operation a century earlier under Andrew Jackson. Farmers in the South and West, for reasons of pure self-interest, voted with the industrial workers of the cities, especially in the East, and voted against the party which traditionally had stood for business and prosperity.

The Republicans did not clearly comprehend the effects of this alignment of farmers and laborers into a unified voting bloc. Even to the extent which they did understand it, the Republicans in Congress split over the measures which had to be designed to wean some members of this coalition away from the Democrats.

It is difficult to establish a rigid group of categories and place each Republican Congressman into one or the other of them. By and large, however, they did fall into three main categories. In the first may be numbered those who came from the conservative areas and were anti-New Deal. Included among this faction were Harold Knutson of Minnesota, Everett Dirksen of Illinois, and Karl Mundt of South Dakota. In the second group, which supported most of the New Deal, were Senators Borah of Idaho, McNary of Oregon, Cutting of New Mexico, and Norris of Nebraska. A third group, which overlapped in many cases with the second, accepted the social and economic reforms of the New Deal, but criticized its methods of administering them. Senators Vandenberg of Michigan and Steiwer of Oregon were the leading exponents of this position.

The Republican split over domestic issues made leadership one of the party's most pressing problems. In 1933, Senator McNary replaced the anti-New Deal Senator James Watson as Republican Senate leader. Representative Snell, a conservative, took over the House Republican leadership, and arch-conservative Henry P. Fletcher was made National Republican Chairman, a post he held until 1936. Representative Snell and Chairman Fletcher were not in accord with the majority of Republicans in Congress, many of whom were voting with the Democrats. The disagreement became public when Senators Borah and Nye in a national radio broadcast condemned Fletcher and ridiculed his statement that Roosevelt was a Marxian radical. Moreover, Borah and Nye advocated a more liberal party which would respond to the demands for social and economic reform. Another advocate of a progressive Republican party, William Allen White, rejoiced over the fact that the Republican reactionaries were being defeated. Colonel Frank Knox, Landon's running mate, called himself a Teddy Roosevelt Republican and as such backed much of the New Deal.

All of the pleas for a more liberal party began to make an impression on the rest of the party. After Landon's 1936 defeat various Republicans began to offer definite ways for the party to meet the Roosevelt challenge. The most prevalent suggestion was that of calling a convention before the 1938 Congressional elections in order to draft a platform. This plan was first suggested by John Hamilton, who had been Landon's campaign manager and who succeeded Henry Fletcher as Republican National Chairman in June of 1936. Hamilton definitely was not a Fletcher Republican. He was, in reality, neither a reactionary nor an opponent of social and economic reform, rather he represented the middle-of-the-road Republicans.

The plan to call a national convention was never carried out. It failed because of the split in the party and/or the fight among the party hierarchy. At this time each of four men considered himself the real leader of the party, and none of them publicly admitted that any of the others had a claim to the title. These four men were: Alf Landon, who believed that he was the head of the party since he was the last Republican candidate for President; Herbert Hoover, who felt that since he was the last man that the party had elected President he should be its spokesman; John Hamilton, who claimed the position by virtue of his job as National Chairman; and Senator Arthur Vandenburg, who, although not the official Republican leader in the Senate, headed the anti-New Deal coalition of Republicans and Democrats.

Despite this leadership fight, the National Committee and prominent Republicans were able to agree that a commission should be established to investigate the social and economic conditions of the country and that this committee should make suggestions for future action. Aside from the establishment of this committee, the Republicans did little from an organizational or an ideological standpoint to liberalize the party or its program.

The committee headed by Dr. Glenn Frank, former president of the University of Wisconsin, was composed of two hundred Republicans representing all levels of government and party organization as well as a broad cross section of American life. The Frank Committee findings and recommendations were issued in 1940 under the title, *A Program for a Dynamic America: Report of the Republican Program Committee.* In essence the report accepted most of the New Deal, with but slight camouflage. The committee could not resist a backward gaze at the halcyon days of normalcy. They suggested that "the largest feasible proportion of relief costs should be borne by the state and localities." After reaffirming their faith in states' rights, the committee temporized on agricultural policy: "A rational farm program will not include acreage control as a permanent policy and will countenance its continuance only until more fundamental policies . . . bring the problem of farm surpluses under control." With paroxysms of regret, the Republicans were tendering grudging homage to the New Deal.

Just as the Republicans were beginning to make their peace with the New Deal on domestic policy, another spectre from the past in the form of international questions demanded their attention. The foreign crisis grew steadily worse throughout the decade, and the serious differences of opinion on domestic policy were added to by the difficulties of securing unity on pressing international problems. During his first administration, Roosevelt, like the majority of the people, was primarily concerned with domestic affairs and devoted little attention to foreign affairs. At the beginning of his second term, the President called for a "quarantine" against the powers disturbing the peace. The public response to this appeal was apathetic despite the realities of the world situation. These realities consisted in the fact that Mussolini had already devoured Ethiopia; Hitler had re-occupied the Rhineland; Italy, Germany, and Soviet Russia were intervening in the Spanish Civil War; and the Japanese armies were invading China. Among the reasons for this apathy were the reports that Republican Senator Nye was making on his "Merchants of Death" investigation. This investigation, a one-man attempt to prove that World War I had been caused by European imperialists, provided great quantities of ammunition for the isolationists.

The foreign affairs problem soon became one of the chief concerns of Congress; however, from 1935 to 1939, Congress debated and passed various pieces of neutrality legislation. The central question throughout this period was whether the United States should sell arms to the belligerent powers. By the end of 1939 the first attempt to solve the problem, the Arms Embargo Act, was repealed, and Congress recognized the necessity of aiding the Allies. The majority of the Republicans in Congress were opposed to the embargo repeal and were for the position of strict neutrality, which meant that they were expressing traditional isolationism. The most vocal members of this group were: Hamilton Fish, ranking Republican on the House Foreign Affairs Committee; Representative Tinkham, second ranking Republican on the House Foreign Affairs Committee; and Senators Vandenberg and Borah who were members of the Senate Foreign Relations Committee. These men and others were able to exert a powerful influence on public opinion. The Senate and the House served as sounding boards from which they could express their isolationist views. Fish, Vanderberg, and Borah were among the Republicans with the most years of Congressional service and, in a sense, were looked upon as party statesmen.

The isolationists in and out of Congress charged that Roosevelt wanted war to spur the economy and prevent the demise of the New Deal. At the beginning of 1940, the Frank Committee predicted the end of "our economic system of free enterprise," as well as "our political system of representative self-government" if we went to war. In strong language the committee contended that "if we participate in this war under the leadership which, in peace time, seeks to centralize virtually all power over the enterprise of the nation . . ., it is reasonable to assume that at the end of the war, such leadership would be reluctant to surrender the powers war had lodged in its hands." The isolationists were dogged in ignoring the spreading shadow of the swastika.

Although not directly represented very heavily in Congress, there was another powerful Republican wing which stood opposed to the isolationists. This wing was composed of the international bankers, traders, and manufacturers who recognized the necessity of maintaining foreign markets. Because of their business connections, this group recognized as early as 1937 the importance of the world conflict. Republican exponents of internationalism date from John Hay, Elihu Root, and

Theodore Roosevelt and carry on through Frank Knox, Henry Stimson, John Foster Dulles, and Henry Cabot Lodge, Jr. As is not unusual in American parties, the views of the Republicans on foreign affairs ranged over the whole scale of possibilities.

A third segment in the party occupied something of an intermediary position between the out-and-out isolationists and the internationalists. Although recognizing the need for home-front preparedness, representatives of this group remained opposed to any steps, such as aid to the Allies, which might lead to war. After Hitler's invasion of Poland in 1939, this faction was greatly enlarged. In fact, many of the former isolationists were forced to adopt a position in support of preparedness because of the immediate dangers resulting from the European war. In 1939, Senator Taft was the outstanding convert to this alignment. Although Taft and other Republicans supported preparedness, they viewed the Selective Service Act of 1940 as an attempt to make the country war-conscious and more willing to enter the European war.

By the end of 1939, then, the Republican party was racked with internal strife. It was disunited on both domestic and foreign affairs. The splits in the party were multiple and more frustrating than usual because many of the economic liberals (mainly agrarians, such as Borah, Nye, Vandenberg, and McNary) were also isolationists. This division within a division prevented the formation of a unified front on both national and international issues by the liberal eastern internationalists and the economically liberal agrarians. With the exception of the agrarians, the isolationists were economic conservatives and most of the internationalists were economic liberals. This curious intransigence of forces served to compound the split within the party.

The many-sided Republican split not only produced a fight for control of the party, but helped to create a vacuum of leadership. This vacuum resulted in part from the fact that the Republicans had lost four straight elections. But the loss of elections was a manifestation of something deeper. Since the President had been able to hold his popular support through seven years of experimentation, there was a strong implication that something was wrong with the opposition. Much uncertainty plagued the Republican party in the late 1930's, and the war in Europe could not entirely account for it. More important was the ambivalence within the country which had grown as a result of the depression and the popular support which sustained the Democrats in their efforts to cope with this economic disaster. It was imperative that the splits on domestic and international policy within the Republican party be cemented and that in cementing them some basis of support belonging to the Democrats be attracted to the Republicans.

One of the main problems of the party was that for seven years it had rallied against one man — Franklin Roosevelt. The conservative element failed to realize that there was more involved than a personality with what they regarded as peculiar economic ideas. The whole world was in a state of economic and social revolution. For the first time in U.S. history the once quiescent mass-man had been injected into the middle of the political arena. The conservative Republicans, although accepting the fact that something could be done to ameliorate the plight of the masses, missed the significance of the movement for social and economic reform. In their bitter attacks on Roosevelt they appeared to oppose the very principle of change.

Scores of commentators offered advice to the Republicans. Two of the most provocative pieces appeared during the summer of 1938. They were written by Margaret Banning, "The Conservative Front," in *The Saturday Evening Post,* and Harold Varney, "What Can the Republicans Do?" in the *American Mercury.* The general tenor of this advice was that the Republicans would have to show not alone in 1940, but in preceding years, that they did not have the limited, selfish, greedy point of view which they were declared to have by their opponents. In effect, the critics of Republicanism were calling for a liberal conservative who could, as it were, catch the Republicans up with the times.

By late 1939, then, it appeared that the Republicans would have to effect some type of alliance between the conservatives and the liberals, the isolationists and the internationalists. In essence, they were faced with the necessity of nominating a man who accepted the principle of social and economic change and at the same time a man who would be able to make some constructive criticisms which would stimulate reaction against New Deal domestic policies. Further, the man would have to take a stand on the international question which would rally the voters and unify the party. The qualifications demanded a man who was cut in the pattern of the times. A month before the 1940 Republican convention such a man appeared in the person of Wendell Willkie. The struggles of the party which revolved around him during the first half of 1940 were a continuation of those which the party had been embroiled in for nearly eight years. With Willkie's victory at the nominating convention, an uneasy and unstable alignment of the factions within the party was achieved.

TAFT, DEWEY, AND VANDENBERG

As soon as Roosevelt was elected in 1936 the Republicans began the search for a presidential candidate. Numerous men were mentioned. But there were three who were continuously thought of as presidential timber and who survived the preliminary weeding out. The three men who emerged in the latter half of 1939 were Senator Robert Taft, District Attorney Thomas Dewey, and Senator Arthur Vandenberg. All had qualifications which were brought to the attention of the people.

Alice Roosevelt Longworth, Teddy Roosevelt's daughter, in an article, "What's the Matter With Bob Taft?" in the May 4, 1940 issue of *The Saturday Evening Post,* seems to have captured much of Taft's appeal when she explained that "I am for Bob Taft because I do not yearn any longer for the man who is always on his toes, waving his hat, raising his voice, raring to go here, there, anywhere." Alice Longworth was certainly right when she said that Bob Taft was not ready to "go here, there, anywhere." If there ever was a man who was consciously aware of every political move he made, it was Bob Taft. He started the "right" political way by working as a precinct committeeman in his home town, Cincinnati, Ohio. After a year's service in this lowly position he was elected to the Ohio State House of Representatives and served as speaker and floor leader. Eight years of hard work and loyal service to the party enabled him to move up to the Ohio Senate. After only one term in the Senate, Taft became a victim of the 1932 Roosevelt landslide. During his tenure as a state legislator he devoted himself to the task of straightening out Ohio's state and municipal borrowing programs and fast gained the reputation as a hard man with the dollar.

Ohio Republicans were proud of Bob Taft, and in 1939 he was their favorite son candidate for the Republican presidential nomination. In 1938, after winning a hard fight from Judge Arthur Day in the United States senatorial primary he defeated the Democratic nominee, Robert

Bulkley, who had President Roosevelt's endorsement. The pattern for the many other campaigns he was to wage was established in the contest with Bulkley. He stated the facts of the issue as he understood them. There was a frigidness in his utterances. This manifested itself in the way he buried himself in a manuscript with a seeming indifference to attempts by the audience to interrupt him with applause.

Upon arrival in the United States Senate, Taft was given membership on three important committees — Banking and Currency, Appropriations, and Labor. This was unusual for a freshman senator but not for Taft. Taft was peculiarly fitted to assume a great share of the Republican Congressional leadership. William S. White, a Taft biographer, explains Taft's prominence by likening him to a refuge where the hardcore Republicans could find safety from the forces which had been unleashed during the New Deal. "Who in these circumstances could overlook Taft of Ohio? There was a famous name redolent of the old, safe days of the Republican party and a name never touched in the remotest ways by the aura of scandal that had arisen during the Harding Administration."

In February, 1939, the presidential talk concerning Taft's possibilities became serious when Arthur Krock called Taft as tough as any candidate the Republicans could offer. In a later column Krock observed that Taft had been industriously assailing spending and lending in a way to attract the favorable attention of his party nationally. A "Taft-for-President Club" was started in Kansas City during June of 1939. The way was cleared for Taft's announcement of his candidacy when Ohio's Governor Bricker revealed that he would seek another gubernatorial term and that he would support Taft for the presidential nomination. On August 3, 1939, a resolution was passed by the Hamilton County Republican Executive Committee urging Taft to allow his name to be used as the first choice of Ohio's delegation to the national convention. The next day Taft issued a statement permitting his name to be placed in nomination.

His announcement was no surprise. Taft had the advantage of being from a pivotal state, Ohio, where seven of the Republican presidents had been born; but more than that, he was an orthodox Republican. Although an intelligent man, he thought in terms of fact which to him had no latitude, longitude nor expansion — you were either right or wrong. Taft lacked glamour and he knew it. One columnist reported an exchange he had with Taft on this subject. "The trouble with glamour," said Taft, "is what's so frequently underneath it." "What?" asked the columnist. "Too little!" replied Taft. *Time* magazine characterized Taft as being "prissy, solemn, and ponderous." Furthermore, he could not boast that he had come "up from nothing." He had had plenty all of his life and was aware of it.

Taft's attraction lay in the fact that he believed in stability, regularity, order, solvency, and tradition. These were the qualities ascribed to Taft, and they were the things in which the traditional Republicans believed. Here was a man to whom the Old Guard could look with hope.

If Taft lacked glamour, Thomas E. Dewey had it in abundance. His was a story that would warm the heart of every American who had read Horatio Alger. Dewey, in contrast with Taft, had been born into a plain, midwestern family. Until he was in his early twenties he had planned a singing career. It was only after he had moved to New York and began studying law at Columbia University that he definitely gave up voice lessons.

Upon graduation from Columbia, Dewey worked in several New York City law firms. His legal work was outstanding and attracted the attention of George Z. Medalie, a distinguished member of the New York Bar. When Medalie was appointed United States Attorney for the Southern District of New York he asked Dewey to join him as his Chief Assistant. Dewey, just twenty-nine at this time, (March 15, 1931), was the youngest man ever to hold this position.

Governor Lehman, after four prominent Republicans had refused, appointed Dewey Special Prosecutor of New York City in May, 1935. This appointment was the beginning of a career which was to make him a national "Mr. District Attorney." In 1937, Dewey was elected District Attorney for New York County. He capitalized on the graft, gangsterism, and corruption that had been plaguing New York. Dewey ran an unsuccessful race against Herbert Lehman for the coveted governorship of New York in 1938; but his gangbusting was more than enough to mark him as a presidential possibility. At thirty-seven, Dewey was waging and winning the war against "sin." His exploits were unequalled in American criminal history. The men and women with whom he tangled read like a national rogue's gallery — Charles Mitchell, Henry Miro, Arthur Flegenheimer (Dutch Schultz), "Waxey" Gordon, "Jennie the Factory," "Gashouse Lil," "Frisco Jean," "Sadie the Chunk," "Lucky" Luciano, Jimmy Hines, and Charles "Tootsie" Herbert. Dewey's activity appealed to the imagination of the people.

In listing the most important news stories of 1938, the Associated Press placed four of Dewey's exploits high on their list — the James J. Hines trial, the Dewey-Lehman campaign, the sentencing of Richard Whitney, and the capture of "Dixie" Davis. The professional politicians, however, were most interested in Dewey's close race against Lehman. Dewey presidential talk began growing as soon as the significance of the 1938 New York vote had seeped throughout the country.

Dewey's decision to seek the nomination was made public on December 1, 1939. He was only thirty-eight at that time, the youngest man to seek a majority nomination since William Jennings Bryan. At first his youth made little difference, although Secretary of Interior Ickes jokingly remarked that Dewey had thrown his diapers into the ring.

Senator Arthur Vandenberg, unlike Dewey and Taft, had been on the national scene for over a decade. He had been elected to the United States Senate in the 1928 Republican sweep. Prior to his entrance into the Senate he had been one of the most successful newspapermen in Michigan. Senator Vandenberg had been talked of as a presidential possibility for years. In 1936, he was mentioned and according to some pundits, might have had the nomination had he sought it seriously.

One thing which seemed to place Vandenberg in an advantageous position was that he had served throughout the New Deal. He had been re-elected to the Senate in the "hard year," 1934. His re-election was due, in part, to the fact that he had supported a good many of the social and economic reform measures of the New Deal. Moreover, the Senator was friendly with the Democratic and Republican Congressional leaders. This was most certainly an advantage over Dewey and Taft. The New Deal had cast a "long shadow" in which the Republicans would have to dwell. Arthur Krock observed as early as May 26, 1939 that Vandenberg was one of the few Republicans who knew his way around in this "shadow." James Reston took a somewhat dimmer view of Vandenberg's chances, because the Senator was on record on too many critical issues. During the course of his long tenure he had alienated powerful groups.

Like Taft and Dewey, Senator Vandenberg let it be known early, that he would accept the Republican presidential nomination. But this willingness to accept was based on several reservations which were to haunt him throughout the campaign for delegates. In a letter to the Kansas Republican State Chairman, Walter Fess, he made his reserved statement. "I do not consider myself to be a candidate in the usual sense of the word. I have indicated my willingness to serve in this terrific responsibility, but I have also indicated that I have absolutely no personal aspirations in this direction and that I shall not personally participate in any preconvention campaign for delegates."

By the middle of January, 1940, then, there were three major candidates for the Republican presidential nomination. All three, before the campaign started, appeared to have about equal strength. Each had definite advantages and drawbacks. Taft, Vandenberg, and Dewey agreed that the next president would have to eliminate waste, cut the federal payroll, trim the power of the bureaucracy, lower taxes, balance the budget, remove some restrictions from business, and encourage business so the whole country would prosper.

In an effort to stir the public, the Republican party sponsored speaking engagements throughout the country for the three aspirants in the first two months of 1940. Moreover, the Republican National Committee, on the advice of its chairman, John Hamilton, asked the various party leaders to make Lincoln Day speeches in all the major United States cities. Among those who made Lincoln Day speeches were Dewey in Portland, Oregon; Taft in Greensboro, North Carolina; John D. Hamilton and Mrs. Taft at the National Republican Club; Herbert Hoover in Omaha; Governor James, Senator Vandenberg and Harold Stassen at Grand Rapids, Michigan; Senator Lodge in Brooklyn; Bruce Barton at Buffalo; Senator Bridges in Oklahoma City; Hanford MacNider at Boston; and Hamilton Fish in Chicago. These speeches were the signal for the campaign to begin in earnest.

Another project which the National Committee backed was an investigation of conditions within the United States. This was the research mentioned previously and carried on by Dr. Frank, former University of Wisconsin president, over a two-year period. Released in February of 1940, the report unfortunately added nothing new in the way of campaign ammunition. In essence the report merely confirmed a situation which had been eloquently indicated by the Republican presidential aspirants. That, with perhaps a few exceptions, the Republican party had not thought of countering the basic purposes of the New Deal. Rather, they were asking for a mandate to change some of the methods which had been used. The candidates made numerous references to the Frank report, but only when it suited their purposes. It had little apparent effect on the 1940 campaign.

After the first feeling-out period — the travel and talk interval — ended, it became apparent that Dewey was to be the early front-runner. Former Governor Alan Fuller of Massachusetts declared that he was supporting Tom Dewey because, as he put it, Dewey was the "Sir Galahad to lead the Republican party to victory." Fuller, attempting to play on what might become a Taft and Vandenberg weakness, recalled that a senatorial cabal brought about the nomination of Warren Harding. This was an indirect shot at the senators. It means that some members of the party were tired of being controlled by the Congressional clique.

To head his campaign, Dewey selected two political veterans, J. Russel Sprague of New York and Ruth Hanna McCormick Simms, the daughter of Mark Hanna. Although Dewey attracted many of the "politicos" he never was able to get the nod from the big four — Herbert Hoover, Joseph Martin, John Hamilton and Alf Landon. Dewey did have some long talks with Hoover. And Hoover agreed with most Republicans in saying that Dewey "had fired the imagination of the American youth." This is as much of an endorsement as Dewey ever received from the ex-President.

Dewey was clearly the favorite in the early months, if the Gallup Poll can be taken as an accurate index of the candidates' strength. For the months of January and March the poll showed the relative rank of the candidates as follows:

	January	March
	PER CENT	PER CENT
Dewey	60	53
Taft	11	17
Vandenberg	16	19
Hoover	5	5
Others	8	6

The Roper Poll conducted for *Fortune* used a different method from that employed by Dr. Gallup. Instead of asking the rank and file Republicans to indicate their choice for the nomination, Roper took a random sample in six sections of the United States and asked people for their preferences in both parties. In other words, Roper asked the Democrats and Republicans to indicate their preference, then he took the total number who gave a Republican or Democratic choice and tried to ascertain the relative strength of the parties. His results differed considerably from Gallup's.

	Per Cent Northeast	Per Cent Midwest	Per Cent Northwest	Per Cent Southeast	Per Cent Southwest	Per Cent Mountain	Per Cent Pacific
Dewey	14	8	10	3	1	11	16
Vandenberg	6	8	5	1	1	1	4
Taft	4	7	5	1	1	1	5
Hoover	3	1	1	1	—	1	4
Others	16	14	25	4	3	14	9

The Gallup Poll indicates that Dewey was the overwhelming favorite in the early months. The Roper Poll did not deny the fact that Dewey was more popular than the other candidates, but it did not give him a clear majority. There is little point in attempting to defend either set of results, but there are two important conclusions that can be drawn from these polls. First, Dewey was ahead in the popularity contest. But in spite of this lead, it is questionable whether the rank and file Republicans would have given Dewey the nomination at this time had there been a national preferential primary.

No one can deny the importance of public opinion; however, there are other important considerations for which there must be an accounting. Washington political gossip in the early part of March, 1940, pictured Dewey as the vice-presidential rather than presidential candidate. Many felt that Dewey had been stepping on the toes of political figures. This reaction on the part of the politicians was normal. The uncertainty of the times made it imperative that no candidate should get so far ahead as to preclude consideration of others who might be more suited for the job in the light of possible future political events.

In the early months while Dewey was travelling far and wide, attempting to get the people behind him, Taft was engaging in less spectacular but more profitable enterprises. He had made extensive trips into the South and had talked with the professionals. There were estimates that Taft had sewed up about three hundred southern and miscellaneous delegates during the first three months of the campaign. Meanwhile, Senator Vandenberg had stuck to his seat in the Senate, making only one political speech in St. Paul on February 11.

Despite all the talk and travel of the aspirants, mainly Taft and Dewey, there was little of a concrete nature that could be said about the campaign at the end of March. It was obvious that there were men ready to relieve Roosevelt of his job, and the possibility of Roosevelt's running for a third term overshadowed all other political speculation. Of those actively seeking to replace Roosevelt, Dewey appeared to hold the edge in popular appeal, but lacked delegates. It was felt that the primaries to be held in April would give some candidates more delegates and serve to boost their campaigns in all respects.

Even the primaries were, however, a doubtful barometer in 1940. In many of the primaries there were favorite son candidates; furthermore, some primaries, as was the case with New York, were not binding on the delegates. Another reason why the 1940 primaries were inconclusive was the reluctance of Taft and Dewey to come to a head-on clash except on their respective terms. As a matter of fact, not one Dewey-Taft primary battle occurred. Senator Vandenberg, on the other hand, was not so fortunate as Taft in avoiding a popular contest. He ran against Dewey in primaries in both Wisconsin and Nebraska.

In preparation for the Wisconsin primary, Dewey made two major speeches, one in St. Louis and another in Chicago before 20,000 aroused Deweyites. The theme of both the speeches was morality in government. Dewey accused the New Deal of gross immorality. He played heavily on his gang-busting experiences and inferred that he could clean up the mess in Washington just like he had handled "Dutch Schultz." Vandenberg did not campaign in Wisconsin, but he had several points in his favor. He had had the Senate sounding board available to him during the 1930's, and had used it to support certain social and economic reform measures which had appealed to the Wisconsin voters for years. As an isolationist, Vandenberg was in tune with the popular sentiment there. Moreover, he came from Michigan which is Wisconsin's neighbor.

Dewey, on the other hand, had in the words of J. Russel Sprague, a "well-perfected organization." Both Ruth Hanna McCormick Simms and Colonel Theodore Roosevelt, Jr. had travelled extensively in Wisconsin making speeches and politicking in general. Dewey made a two-day speaking tour in the state after his St. Louis and Chicago appearances.

The big question in Wisconsin was the attitude of the Progressives. Senator LaFollette, a close friend of Senator Vandenberg, did not side with either candidate. However, the Progressive Club of Wisconsin gave its support to Dewey. This organization was not the Progressive party and in order to avoid confusion the Progressive party denied ever having advocated Dewey. The semi-official news organ of the party, *The Madison Capital Times,* condemned the Democratic slate of delegates but pointed out that all those who favored Roosevelt could vote for him since he was running in the preference primary. In Wisconsin a candidate can enter either the delegate or preference primary. President Roosevelt entered the preferential, while Dewey and Vandenberg were entered in the delegate primary. The Progressives, by virtue of this arrangement, could register their approval of Roosevelt without accepting the Democratic delegates.

To offset the Dewey whirlwind campaign, Senator Gerald Nye urged the Progressives to vote for delegates pledged to Senator Vandenberg. Nye went so far as to say that the late Senator Borah, a Progressive, had intended to support Vandenberg, even to the extent of making a nominating speech for him. Senator Nye's plea apparently had little influence on the Progressives or any other voters in Wisconsin. The Wisconsin Republicans elected a full slate of Dewey delegates. The results in the Wisconsin primary demonstrated that Dewey's remarkable run against Governor Lehman in 1938 was neither a fluke nor a register of protest, but proved that he possessed enduring and general vote-getting powers.

In reality, Dewey's Wisconsin victory proved more than his vote-getting ability. It put Senator Vandenberg's candidacy in grave jeopardy unless he could win in Nebraska. Equally important, Dewey's backers were heartened and the weak sisters were encouraged to stay in the Dewey camp, and this made Dewey, in spite of his youth, a serious contender. Moreover, the primary proved the value of a well-financed organization. In some quarters, despite Vandenberg's advantages, Dewey was said to have defeated a straw man, because Vandenberg waged no campaign and had little or no organized support.

The Nebraska preference primary, the only other primary where any of the major Republican contenders met, for all practical purposes put the finishing touches on the death blow that had been dealt to Vandenberg in Wisconsin. In an effort to stave off a total defeat for Vandenberg, Senators Capper of Kansas and McNary of Oregon sent telegrams to Charles A. Reed, Nebraska State Republican Chairman, in which they cited Vandenberg's outstanding record in the Senate. Both Capper and McNary said that the farmer could put his confidence in Vandenberg. Once again, though, Dewey's smooth-running organization combined with his personal appeal proved to be too much for a non-campaigning Senator Vandenberg. Dewey was a decisive four to three winner.

On the same day as the Nebraska primary, Dewey, without opposition, picked up 977,000 votes in the Illinois *advisory* primary. Hamilton Fish had announced in February that he would enter the Illinois primary and run on the issue "Americanism Against Internationalism," but in keeping with the general Republican policy to avoid primary battles he withdrew.

When Mayor LaGuardia of New York learned that a petition had been filed for him to enter the Illinois primary he said in characteristic language: "Tell them for me that I went to see a picture of 'Abe Lincoln in Illinois,' and I looked over the present crop of Republican candidates and I said — Phooey!" He asked that his name be withdrawn because he did not want to split the Progressive vote and explained that President Roosevelt was the candidate for whom Illinois Progressives could vote.

More important in aiding Dewey's cause than the primary victories he won was the fact that Senator Taft would not enter the Maryland primary. J. Russel Sprague challenged Taft to meet Dewey in that primary. Taft asked for time to consider. For many hours he publicly debated and conferred, having, as it were, invited the whole world to witness his hesitation. Instead of accepting the challenge, or immediately saying he would not, Senator Taft followed his own simple and candid ways. At length, he announced in effect since he could not carry Maryland because of Mr. Dewey's foreclosures there, he would not try. Taft's refusal to enter the Maryland primary was recognition of the fact that Dewey was the popular front runner and that he did not care to suffer a defeat similar to that of Senator Vandenberg.

It is not difficult to establish the specific time at which Dewey's popular appeal reached its zenith. Evidently it was immediately after the Wisconsin, Nebraska, and Illinois primaries. A Gallup poll which was conducted in the middle of April lists the position of the Republican candidates in this order:

	April
	PER CENT
Dewey	67
Taft	12
Vandenberg	14
Hoover	2
Others	5

This is a fourteen-point increase over Dewey's March total.

The *Pathfinder* Poll gave Dewey 51.9 per cent of the rank and file Republican support. Previously the *Chicago Tribune* poll had indicated that Dewey was the choice of 55.6 per cent of its Republican readers. It appears as though this upswing in the Dewey boom was a result of the desire for a winner. On April 15, 1940, the *New York Times* reported, "With this feeling prevalent [desire for a winner] among the rank and file Republicans Mr. Dewey stepped out as the 'man on horseback.' "

Of all the candidates Senator Taft was the most outspoken on domestic issues. Time after time, he hammered away at the New Deal's spending policy. In January, 1940, President Roosevelt sarcastically challenged Taft to specify how he would balance the budget, and offered Taft a handsome prize if he could show how this could be done. Taft answered Roosevelt promptly. He said that the budget could be balanced by doing the following:

1. Cut those on relief from 1,300,000 to 750,000.
2. Cut all business-regulating agencies to the barest minimum.
3. Reduce the farm support program.
4. Halt all grants for local public works.

5. Reduce the subsidies to housing and industry.
6. Cut national defense spending.

At Swarthmore College, Taft said that the government could encourage business by "revision of the regulatory measures . . . and by revision of the tax system to encourage thrift, investment and production." Later in the campaign he became more specific about the taxes which he would reduce or eliminate: "The pay-roll tax is particularly oppressive on industry. Yet in the end it is a consumption tax, increasing the taxes of every wage earner as well as employer directly or through increase in the cost of his food and clothing. It puts a premium on getting rid of employers and increasing unemployment." Taft said that a sales tax would be much better; furthermore, he urged a reduction in the capital gains tax.

Senator Taft was wise enough to realize that all of the New Deal measures could not be repealed. In Miami, Florida, speaking on the subject "What Should the Republican Party Do If It Is Returned to Power?" he contended that: "It must and should afford adequate relief to the poor. It must and should assist the farmer, whose prices are far below what they ought to be in proportion to city wages and industrial prices. It must and should continue reasonable old age pensions and unemployment insurance . . . All these things can be done. They can be done more economically, and more efficiently than under the present system."

In advocating a retention of these social and economic reforms, Taft's position was similar to that of Dewey and Vandenberg. Vandenberg, as has been mentioned previously, supported many of the New Deal measures. Dewey, likewise, in a speech in Indianapolis, Indiana, recognized the necessity for such things as social security, unemployment insurance, maintenance of adequate agricultural prices, etc. But in that same speech he offered his own seven-point program:

1. Demand a national administration that will not look on all business as the enemy.
2. Reduce federal employees.
3. Put experience, ability, and fair play into the Securities and Exchange Commission.
4. Reduce taxes.
5. Encourage new commercial banks.
6. Put an end to government experimentation.
7. Learn the difference between stopping abuse and grabbing power.

These were the domestic policies which Dewey advocated throughout his campaign.

Unfortunately, this somewhat liberal economic position of the candidates was obscured by their constant attacks on Roosevelt and the New Deal. They spent far more time in criticism and in assuming a negative attitude than in offering a positive program. Taft said that the continuance of the New Deal meant the choking of industrial enterprises. He felt that industry would never expand again. "It [the New Deal] means continued depression and stagnation and in time, a totalitarian state." Here, then, was a tremendous problem. How could one be for government aid to the old, the unemployed, the ill-fed, and the poorly housed and at the same time denounce the very administration which was doing these things? It was a contradiction which the American people could not understand, and, perhaps, one of which the candidates themselves were never fully cognizant.

Dewey was confronted with this dilemma. He characterized the New Deal in the following manner: "For in the past seven years the hand of government has slipped sometimes stealthily and oft times openly into every aspect of our lives. Your stores, your mines, your farms, your smelters, your factories, your railroads — in each the government is demanding and obtaining a greater share of income and control." Dewey, like the others, was not able to offer a program which would continue the social and economic reforms of the New Deal and at the same time eliminate the abusive aspects of too much government.

Senator Vandenberg, although at that time more of an economic and social liberal than either Taft or Dewey, could not resist the temptation to get in a few licks at the program which he had supported. In typical Vandenberg style, he said: "The American people are tired of life on a flying trapeze, and tired of bureaucrats, boon-dogglers, barnacles, brain trusts, ballyhoo, and bankruptcy."

It is not difficult to understand why the American people had grave doubts concerning the Republicans. To be sure, a majority of the people probably disliked part of the New Deal. But, nonetheless, they were reluctant to accept as a possible presidential candidate anyone who would take them back to the Hoover days. And from the position of the three Republican presidential hopefuls this seemed to be a definite possibility. The other Republican leaders recognized this factor; and the effect that the stand of the candidates had on segments within their own party was important in securing the nomination. Throughout the early months of the campaign many of the Eastern Republicans were searching for a candidate who was a little more of a social and economic liberal.

Other forces, too, were at work, creating grave doubts concerning the fitness of the major candidates. As the United States began to get back on its economic feet the attention of the people turned to the events in Europe and Asia. Despite all of the interest that was displayed in the European war, it was still remote. As late as May 10, 1940, David Lawrence could contend: "American isolationism remains the dominant philosophy of the hour. The struggle for human liberty is still academic, remote and intangible so far as it concerns the readiness of American youth to make the supreme sacrifice in the cause of freedom."

Although isolationism was a sacred tenet to many, it began to lose its value as a practical approach to the foreign problem when on April 9, 1940, Hitler's armies struck the Scandinavian countries. Hitler's move was timed perfectly with the Illinois and Nebraska primaries. Nearly all the commentators immediately realized the significance of this historical accident. Many of them argued that the outcome of the presidential primaries in Nebraska and Illinois seemed trivial when compared with what was happening to personal liberty and democracy in Europe. Arthur Krock called upon Dewey to make clear his views on foreign policy.

All other issues were overshadowed rapidly by this change in the European war. Taft and Vandenberg, like Dewey, were asked to state their views on foreign affairs. As the war became more serious, the repercussions on the political availability of the candidates became critical. Unfortunately, the presidential aspirants found it difficult to express their views on foreign affairs in specific terms. The reason for this was that the multiplicity of sectional prejudices and convictions was much more distinct on matters of foreign than on domestic policy. No candidate could possibly have charted the steps we should have taken in advance; the contingencies which were to arise could not have been determined. The Republicans began to weigh the possible effect that the war would have on the November election. They were confronted with the possibility that the Allies might be defeated and this was the toughest aspect of the whole question of campaign strategy.

From Roosevelt's famous "quarantine" speech to Hitler's invasion of the Scandinavian countries, the President gradually had been assuming a more belligerent attitude towards Germany and Italy. Public opinion was not definite on this point. There was a small group which opposed the President while another, and probably smaller, group felt that Roosevelt was not providing the Allies with sufficient encouragement and assistance. During this period, most people seemed to be indifferent to the foreign situation. Many Republican congressional leaders took the opportunity to criticize the chief executive's words and actions. This criticism was in line with the general strategy of opposing the President at every turn.

Dewey, on January 20, 1940, was close to Roosevelt's position in condemning dictatorship. But on the same day he commented: "If there is one thing upon which we are all agreed, it is that we shall send no American to die on the battlefields of Europe." He also blasted the President's earlier recognition of Russia and pointed out that we did not need any "fuzzy departure from the established course of our foreign policy."

During his trip to isolationist Wisconsin, Dewey went isolationist with a big "I." He insisted that any additional aid to the Allies would lead to United States involvement. "I am convinced," said Dewey, "that the only way this country can remain genuinely neutral is for the government to give its full attention to procuring domestic recovery and to keep its hands wholly out of a European war and out of any negotiations that may take place between the warring nations."

No doubt, Dewey's position was created out of expediency. This point was made very clear in an exchange between Tinkham and Sprague. In a speech before the National Republican Women's Club, Tinkham, an isolationist, said that Dewey was unfit to be a candidate for President because of his lack of "sympathy with traditional American policy." J. Russel Sprague quickly retorted that, "Mr. Dewey's sympathy with the objective of the real Republican leadership of Congress is well known and his opposition to foreign entanglements has been stated repeatedly in public." Dewey, therefore, was forced to back the isolationist position to the hilt if he was to get any aid from the isolationist members of Congress.

The war became more intense on May 10 when Germany invaded the "low countries." The British cabinet fell. Chamberlain resigned, and Winston Churchill took over. In view of Dewey's pronouncements, these European developments served to set back his prospects. His youth and inexperience had been raised as objections during the early part of the campaign, but they became much more vulnerable as the gravity of the European war was spotlighted in the press and radio.

Another objection to Dewey was raised about this time. How could he get the nomination without the backing of some congressmen? He had not had any backing from this crucial area early in the campaign. Even though his advisors thought it would eventually come as a result of favorable public response, this Congressional backing never did materialize. Turner Catledge commented: "His [Dewey's] vocal backers in either House of Congress are extremely few. If there is a senator strongly for him, that senator has yet to come forward."

But all of these difficulties did not change Dewey's attitude on foreign policy. In Indianapolis on April 16, he warned against direct or indirect participation, saying that we must even consider the words we use lest they be aggressive. At Oklahoma City he reiterated his stand and said that "the pledge to keep us out of war is one which admits no temporizing." These isolationist speeches brought strong rebukes from President Roosevelt and James Byrnes. Roosevelt said: "I do not subscribe to the preachment of a Republican aspirant who tells you in effect that the United States should do nothing to bring about a better order, a more secure world order of peace." Byrnes charged Dewey with reckless and irresponsible speeches saying that he was using foreign policy to promote his personal ambitions.

In Dallas on May 28, Dewey did change his tune to some degree and advocated aid to the Allies. He still had not been completely converted and added certain reservations to his advocacy. He said that we had resolved, after World War I, not to send any boys to die on foreign soil again. "That decision," he continued, "was made in the calm thoughtfulness of a period of peace and not under the stress of emotions; I for one, stand by that decision." William Allen White, the conscience of the Republican party, noted Dewey's shift: "Mr. Dewey in his early campaign speeches, notably in Wisconsin, where there is a large German element, seemed to be veering toward the isolationists. He seemed against the Allied cause. In a speech in Dallas he retreated to the Allied trenches. And the odd part of it is that his equivocation in Wisconsin was too obvious for too many people for the Dallas speech to make the impression that it deserved."

Dewey's last utterance of the campaign on foreign policy was an attempt to recall to the public the thing that had brought him fame — his gang-busting activities. "As a nation we must face a bitter truth: this has become a gangster world. I know something about gangsters. I know that soft-minded men and guns on order are no help against them. I know that tough-minded men and adequate weapons are the only defense which they respect." This, then, was Dewey's parting appeal to the people. It was true that he had learned much about campaigning, and when to take a stand on issues, but he had learned many of his lessons too late.

The Gridiron Club caught many of Dewey's mistakes in a burlesque of him when a young lad dressed in a little Lord Fauntleroy costume said the following lines:

> N'ya, N'ya, N'ya, I'm the wonder boy,
> N'ya, N'ya, you can't catch me
> N'ya, N'ya, N'ya, I'm the glamour boy — Infant prodegee.
> On each fine speech I work for weeks,
> Casting a binding spell;
> I want a chance to wear long pants and give the New Deal Hell.
> N'ya, N'ya, N'ya, I'm the foxy boy,
> N'ya, N'ya, you can't catch me,
> N'ya, N'ya, N'ya, I'm the pretty boy,
> Where's the White House key?
> Oh, Washington needs me!

Dewey's stand on foreign affairs in part resulted in the loss of a powerful supporter, Kenneth F. Simpson, Republican National Committeeman from New York. Simpson was characterized as an undiplomatic, redheaded Irishman who was too liberal for Dewey's right wing. Simpson had managed Dewey's 1938 campaign for governor and was one of his first advisers. But early in 1940 it became obvious that Simpson was not a last-ditch Dewey man. In fact, on January 16, the Republicans of New York's Seventeenth Assembly District voted to instruct its delegates to the national convention to vote for Dewey on the first ballot and to follow the lead of Simpson on subsequent ballots. Of course, this was a vote of no confidence in Dewey and he resented it. Toward the end of March, the *New York Times* reported that Simpson was not really for Dewey's nomination, and went on to say that a showdown between the two was imminent.

The New York State Republican Convention met on April 12 and 13. At that meeting Edwin Jaeckle, a Dewey supporter, was elected state chairman. Furthermore, the convention adopted a resolution calling for the election of national committeemen prior to the national convention. This latter move was a direct attack on Simpson, since the national committeemen were always selected during the national convention.

Warren Moscow, *New York Times* writer, says that the complete break between Dewey and Simpson was a result of the intensification of the European war. Simpson, as an internationalist, could not agree with Dewey's isolationist stand and had made his position public. On the other hand, Dewey, bolstered by primary victories, decided to consolidate his strength in his home state. Dewey understandably was anxious to have Simpson out before the convention. Simpson anticipated his ouster and began to attack Dewey openly: "What infinite patience, temperateness, and adaptability will be required of our next President.

Then there will be no room for the principle of purge or the frame of mind that lies behind it." After one of Simpson's associates, Raymond Fanning, accused Jaeckle of using "Hitleresque" tactics in purging the party, Jaeckle asserted that Simpson was applying his usual "wolf in sheep's clothing" methods. Jaeckle further stated that the Republican party could not tolerate any Trojan horses.

After a series of these vituperative exchanges, the New York, Dewey-dominated, Republican State Committee met and voted to oust Simpson. Simpson fought against this move and was supported by Frank E. Gannett, wealthy New York newspaper publisher, who was a minor candidate for the Republican nomination. After his defeat Simpson issued a simple statement, an indication of what would happen at the Convention. "We have," said Simpson, "lost the first battle. We will win the next at Philadelphia . . . My defeat in this preliminary battle has focused attention on the more and more apparent absurdity of nominating Mr. Dewey." Stanley Walker, Dewey's sympathetic biographer, tries to explain the Simpson defection in terms of Simpson's personality by saying that he was "moody, depressed, or choleric." But Simpson's break with Dewey went much deeper than mere personalities. Simpson was, as an economic liberal, dissatisfied with Dewey's domestic policies. But more important, Simpson recognized that the United States could never be led by an isolationist, and he was convinced that Dewey had bound himself to that position.

By the middle of June, Dewey's bandwagon possibilities were greatly diminished. In April, after the primaries, Dewey reached his peak. His decline may be attributed to the fact that as the foreign situation became critical, Dewey's isolationist stand, combined with his youth and inexperience, became handicaps. Also, Vandenberg, although not campaigning, refused to quit, and Taft had been quietly successful in lining up delegates. Dewey's difficulties with the New York delegation did not set well with professionals throughout the country. And as the Dewey bandwagon began to stall, the Willkie boom was beginning to take on serious proportions.

Taft, Dewey's closest rival prior to the convention, did not achieve a national following. According to the Gallup poll he never had the backing of more than 17 per cent of the rank and file Republicans. Taft was not a colorful personality. In fact, he almost fitted the stereotype which he was supposed to represent — the calm and cool conservative. Taft's drabness was offset to some degree by his wife. Martha Bowers Taft was an energetic campaigner. In the 1938 Ohio senatorial campaign she travelled throughout the state with her husband, and spoke with disarming frankness. In 1938, while addressing a group of coal miners, she said: "My husband is not a simple man. He did not start from humble beginnings. My husband is a brilliant man. He had a fine education . . . He has been trained well for the job. Isn't that what you want when you pick a man to work for you?" She had little to do with the strategy of the campaign, serving only as a strong propagandist of a cause.

In 1940, Martha Taft picked up where she had left off in 1938. This time, however, she was stumping the whole country. Typical of her speeches were those delivered before the National Republican Club on Lincoln's birthday and an impromptu speech before the Twelfth Assembly District Club in New York City. She was the only wife of a candidate who actively campaigned.

From all indications Martha Taft's campaign activities were colorful and politically advantageous. Her husband, however, was not so fortunate. The first serious blunder that Taft committed was in a speech before the Gridiron Club, which he read in a dull monotone without ever stopping for applause. Furthermore, the speech was full of dry statistics. It was just the kind of speech the august, not-too-long-hairish Gridiron Club did not want to hear.

Time awarded Taft the prize for the "most courageous, most politically inept campaign statement." This award was given for Taft's blunt announcement in Des Moines, Iowa, that he whole-heartedly opposed the New Deal's corn-loan policy. On the very day of his statement the Agriculture Department issued a fifty-seven cent per bushel loan, thus pouring about $70 million into the Corn State. He also made other costly blunders. One week later, (December 8, 1939), in Kansas City he crossed a picket line and a precedent to the effect that politicians never cross such lines. The American Federation of Labor had been picketing the Kansas City Club for a year. In Texas while on vacation Taft shot his first wild turkey. He was photographed in a business suit gingerly holding the dead bird, a picture that must have brought a series of nostalgic memories of Calvin Coolidge.

Despite, or perhaps because of, his drabness, Taft did pick up delegate strength prior to the convention. He travelled throughout the country talking to the political bosses. His aim, for the most part, was not to secure delegate pledges; rather it was to recruit the implicit support of the uninstructed delegations. His advisers believed that he was gaining in popular appeal and that the only way this could be translated into delegate support was through an open and free convention — one that was willing to listen to the party's Old Guard leaders.

Moreover, Taft felt the convention would reject Dewey on the grounds that he was a newcomer.

This fight between the Taft Old Guard and Dewey was important, and as the campaign progressed Taft and Dewey began to point their guns at each other. Dewey, according to Taft supporters, had been exaggerating his delegate strength. Taft headquarters issued a statement to counter the Dewey claims. The gist of the statement was that:

1. Taft would have strength in every state.
2. In the South, Frank Gannett would have more delegates than Dewey.
3. Taft would have more delegates than Dewey.
4. Taft would be nominated.

Taft was attempting to stop Dewey and was willing to join with candidates like Gannett to do this. It can also be said that Dewey looked upon Taft as the first man that he had to beat. By virtue of their not-too-secret hostility for one another, Taft and Dewey were compounding the conditions which would force the convention to choose another candidate.

It appeared that Taft was gaining on Dewey during the first part of May. In Indiana and the ten other states he visited at that time, he learned that his stock was mounting daily. He discovered also the uncertainties and the concomitant feeling that a man of experience and stability was preferred by many, particularly the political leaders. Taft also gained the support of a powerful element in the business community when the 1940 convention of the Chamber of Commerce took a wholly unofficial and sudden practical political turn. Seventy-five to a hundred of the delegates slipped quietly out for an off-the-record conference with Taft, after which they gave him their endorsement.

Notwithstanding Taft's support by political leaders and influential businessmen, he was in virtually the same position as Dewey with respect to foreign affairs. His deepest conviction was that nothing could be gained by an embroilment of the United States. Taft was, however, one of the eight senators who voted against the Arms Embargo Act on the basis that "embargos nullify rather than promote neutrality."

Throughout the campaign Taft espoused the doctrine of preparedness. In February, when others were circumventing the issue, Taft spoke with his usual candor. "Prepare adequately for defense, but keep out of war. America cannot live within a Chinese wall, but it can shape its own policy to keep out of war." His views on preparedness began to appear as attacks on the Administration. And questions arose as to just how much defense he thought necessary. Taft held to the position that the President was not accepting the idea of the people "that we must stay out of war except a war of defense."

While Taft was touring the Midwest in May he was told that affairs in Europe had dampened the ardor for Mr. Dewey. In spite of this, and in spite of warnings from Alf Landon and Republican leaders for eight other states that sympathy for the Allies was mounting daily, Taft exhorted the country to keep its mind on domestic affairs. "This is," he said, "no time for the people to be wholly absorbed in foreign battles simply because the newspapers with screaming headlines devote the first three pages exclusively to news from Europe." That this attitude was contrary to the sentiment of the area is unquestionable. It was reported that no less than fifty influential Republican leaders told Taft that the people were for the Allies short of war. Yet, Taft was frankly negative on the foreign question. He gave the impression that it did not make any difference who won the war.

Senator Vandenberg had the distinction of being the arch-isolationist among the big three Republican presidential aspirants. His aversion to war began early and continued to grow throughout the campaign. In his Lincoln Day address Senator Vandenberg gave the theme of his position. "Stay out of war, quarantine the third term-ites, and then watch the country boom." Instead of advocating aid to the Allies as Dewey finally did, or recognizing that war could come and that we must be prepared for it as Taft did, Vandenberg held to a policy of insulation. "We must never," he said, "surrender to the state of mind which resigns itself to the inevitability of our involvement — a state of mind which entirely too often possesses Washington."

Vandenberg felt that there was no justification for policies which would threaten our neutrality. He believed that the place to "save democracy" was at home. His marked departure from the other candidates was his view concerning the possible results of the war. "America," he stated, "is not automatically lost if the Allies lose . . . our prospectus must contemplate our ability to survive regardless of who wins the war in Europe." Obviously Vandenberg's policy of insulation was in complete accord with the traditional isolationist point of view, if not, in some cases, more extreme.

It is interesting to note that both Taft and Vandenberg took a position different from this with regard to Asia. They were especially concerned over the possibility of losing the Dutch East Indies because the key industries of Ohio and Michigan needed rubber. They made no comment when Secretary of State Hull emphasized the necessity of protecting this vital area. In effect, they were placed in the position of being interventionists in Asia and isolationists in Europe. This contradiction did not worry either; furthermore, it did not seem to affect the public since the real battle was taking place in Europe.

Aside from Vandenberg's contra-public opinion on foreign affairs, there was the fact that he did not campaign for the nomination. In a letter to Lieutenant-Governor Walter S. Goodland of Wisconsin, Vandenberg outlined his reasons for refusing to engage in the scramble for delegates. He said that his primary responsibility was on the floor of the Senate where he was a member of the Finance and Foreign Relations committees. Vandenberg did indicate that if the convention chose him he would enter the campaign with every resource and energy at his disposal. Regardless of the Senator's motives, the American people were witnessing one of the most heated campaigns for delegates in the history of our country. Vandenberg by choosing to remain in the Senate, was not given as much publicity as his rivals. It is difficult to say how much participation would have helped him, but it is fair to say that non-involvement hindered him.

There was a host of minor candidates for the Republican nomination in 1940. Most of them were "favorite sons" or men who thought that they could get the nomination if the convention were to become deadlocked. In fact, almost every important Republican was mentioned. The men who were most frequently mentioned included: Governor Raymond Baldwin of Connecticut; Henry Cabot Lodge and Leverett Saltonstall of Massachusetts; W. Warren Barbour, Frank Gannett, and Bruce Barton of New York; Senator Styles Bridges of New Hampshire; Supreme Court Justice Owen J. Roberts; Governor Arthur James of Pennsylvania; Senator Charles McNary of Oregon; Senator Hanford MacNider of Iowa; former President Herbert Hoover; Governor John Bricker of Ohio; House Minority Leader Joseph Martin; Alfred Landon; Homer Capehart of Indiana; Colonel Frank Knox, Landon's running mate in 1936; and New York City's Mayor LaGuardia.

Frank Gannett, New York newspaper publisher, was the only one of these minor candidates who carried on an active campaign. Gannett made as many speeches as Taft or Dewey. He toured the country in his private airplane and gave numerous speeches before country club groups, Chambers of Commerce and Rotary clubs. In all of his public utterances Gannett adhered to the conservative point of view. He condemned the New Deal in totality and was against aid to the Allies. Because of his stand on issues and his natural colorlessness, Gannett never attracted much attention or support on a national basis.

Nonetheless, Gannett did present a special problem to Dewey. In

1938, the Association of Rural Counties was founded out of the dissatisfaction with Dewey. It was composed of a group of leaders from western and central New York state and was the group behind Gannett. In essence, the Gannett movement was a reaction to Dewey. In an attempt to mollify the Gannett forces Dewey leaders agreed to give them one of New York's delegates-at-large. The truce that resulted from this compromise was short-lived. Gannett joined forces with Simpson which was an obvious matter of political expediency because the liberal Simpson and the conservative Gannett held only one position in common, that of being opposed to Dewey's nomination. This split in the New York delegation was to have serious repercussions in the convention.

Thus far, only the activities of the orthodox Republican aspirants have been discussed. The handicaps of these candidates were minor compared with those of Wendell L. Willkie, the most unusual prospect for a major party nomination. But unlike the other candidates Willkie's apparent drawbacks, paradoxical as it might seem, became advantages by convention time.

Messner in the Rochester Times-Union

"On His Way"

THE IMMORTAL AMATEUR

Wendell Willkie has been characterized as the "Immortal Amateur." In this respect, Willkie's role in American history is fascinating. He was an amateur in business and was not a politician in the usual sense of the word. Willkie was both an unusual man and an unusual candidate for the Republican presidential nomination in 1940.

In 1918, Willkie wanted to run for Congress on the Democratic ticket. He asked a friend and old Indiana politician, Frank C. Dailey, whether he should enter the political arena. Dailey, according to Joseph Barnes, a Willkie biographer, told him in all frankness: "I think you are the God-damndest stupidest man in Indiana. Sure you'll win, with a war record. But you'll lose your practice. And you'll come back after a couple of years and be just another political lawyer in an Indiana county seat. Listen, Wendell, you've got to go places." What had made Dailey tell Willkie that he should not run for Congress? The answer to this question is buried in Willkie's formative years.

Wendell Willkie was a second-generation American, and family background was very influential in shaping his thinking. His four grandparents had been refugees from German oppression. Given this family history, Willkie could scarcely avoid being molded in a free-lance tradition. His grandparents settled in Elwood, Indiana, and it was there that Wendell was born in 1892. Both of his parents were lawyers, and it is generally believed that his mother was the first woman ever admitted to the Indiana Bar.

Willkie followed in his parents' footsteps and entered Indiana University. Before he received a degree he had harvested wheat in Minnesota, dressed tools in Texas oil fields, operated a cement block machine in Wisconsin, picked vegetables in California, and taught school in Kansas. These experiences were valuable additions to those which he had while still at home. In his college career proper he was an outstanding debater, president of the Jackson Democratic Club, and organizer of the Barbarians (an anti-fraternity group). In politics during his college years, he was regarded by his classmates as a red hot socialist.

Although strongly against fraternities Willkie joined one in the last month of his senior year at Indiana. This was a difficult compromise for him to make, but it had to be done. He told a friend that, "If I don't join Beta, I'll lose my girl, and if I do join, I'll lose my soul." He later married the girl for whom he had given up his soul: Edith Wilk, the Rushville, Indiana assistant librarian.

After receiving his B.A. degree, Willkie went to law school and in 1916 was graduated at the top of his class. His oration at the law school commencement was an attack on the Indiana state constitution, which shocked some members of the faculty and is still remembered at Indiana for its boldness. After law school he joined the Army and served throughout World War I. He attained the rank of captain.

It was upon Willkie's return from the Army, that Frank Dailey, in the talk previously reported, advised him not to run for Congress. Apparently Dailey was aware of the free-lance thinking that young Willkie had been doing. But Dailey did not leave him in the lurch. He gave Willkie a letter to Harvey Firestone, the young Akron, Ohio industrialist, who made Willkie a member of Firestone's legal department. Shortly after arriving in Akron, Willkie left Firestone and joined the law firm of Mather and Nesbitt. The firm was retained by many corporations. Willkie became their trial lawyer and rapidly gained a reputation as one of the best in Ohio. In 1927, at the age of thirty-five, Willkie became a director of the Ohio State Bank and the Northern Ohio Power Company. It was this latter position which was destined to have so much influence in taking him to New York.

Throughout this period Willkie considered himself a New Freedom Democrat and as such, supported many of the policies of Woodrow Wilson. In 1924, as a delegate to the Democratic national convention, he was primarily concerned with getting the convention to adopt a resolution condemning the Ku Klux Klan. The Klan fight was not new to him — he had led the fight to keep the Klan out of the Akron School Board. Subsequently, Willkie was a delegate to the 1928 and 1932 Democratic national conventions and supported Newton D. Baker. Baker, like Willkie, was a Wilson Democrat.

Willkie's private life in Akron was not filled with the activities that are generally associated with his generation. According to Barnes, "Golf, bridge, automobiles, the correct political connections, the socially and professionally useful friends — no novel about his generation would be acceptable as credible without these, but none of them plays any part in the record of Willkie's life in Akron." Despite his unique life Willkie was thought of as a plain and simple Hoosier. Booth Tarkington felt that Willkie was "a type familiar to us, a man wholly natural in manner, ... in a word, a man as American as the courthouse in the square of an Indiana county seat. This is, we saw a good, sturdy plain, able Hoosier — and as we ourselves were native Hoosiers we instantly felt that we knew him." But this picture of Willkie is an allegory which glosses over the struggle that had occurred in the United States and which had manifested itself in men like Willkie. This struggle was a result of the industrial revolution and the attempts to solve the problems which it created. It did not give us "good, sturdy, plain and able Hoosiers," but rather men who were filled with a complexity of fears and frustrations.

Willkie realized the struggle in American life. He said, when talking about his home town: "The story of Elwood is the story of America and its problems. It's the perfect laboratory. I've always wanted to write the story myself." He felt that Elwood's economic collapse at the beginning of the twentieth century was based on two factors, "profligate waste of natural resources and over-industrialization." The Elwood experience demonstrated to Willkie "that individuals cannot carry through large-scale social adjustments — that society owes an obligation to its members when it leads them up a blind alley." In essence, Willkie was saying that the agricultural frontier was gone and that machines and cities were creating a new American way of life. He realized, as much as anybody, that there was still a lot of the past left in men. The two towns, Elwood and Rushville, which Willkie regarded as homes, "were committed to the long and uncertain gamble of trying to marry their pioneer, agricultural past with a new capitalistic future."

Russell Davenport, one of Willkie's closest friends, felt as though Willkie's entire life was an ordeal. Davenport calls him the protagonist of a gigantic drama. The dynamic of the ordeal, according to Davenport, was that Willkie could never accept the "status quo" of either Hoover or Roosevelt. Although Willkie lived through both the period of normalcy and of the New Deal, neither social philosophy answered for him the question of how freedom is achieved. "These questions," said Davenport, "of human freedom, specifically in a technological age, were Wendell Willkie's questions." In reality, Willkie was a product of the times. He emerged out of a crisis. Davenport says that "if the people of the future do not know him, they will not know us."

During the Akron years, the struggle in American life had become meaningful to Willkie. He was losing some of his earlier socialist ideas and becoming more and more involved with big business. Due to his work with Mather and Nesbitt he was invited by Bernard Cobb, president of Commonwealth and Southern — a public utilities holding company — to join John C. Weadock who was Commonwealth and Southern's legal representative. This was a few months before the 1929 crash. Because of his outstanding work with Weadock, when Bernard Cobb became chairman of the board of Commonwealth and Southern, Willkie was offered and accepted the presidency of the utilities holding company. He had served in this capacity for only a few months when Cobb had a nervous breakdown. Willkie retained the presidency but declined the board chairmanship. Willkie, at forty-one, was the youngest chief executive officer of a utilities holding company.

The depression of the 1930's had seen business portrayed at its worst. Business leaders of the past were no longer looked upon as protagonists of American life. Moreover, the business community was racked with internal dissension. Businessmen were finding it difficult to defend their cause, and these were the years when there was a marked vacuum of leadership of the anti-New Deal coalition of business men. It was in this situation that Wendell Willkie found himself. He needed no urging to assume a great share of the leadership.

Two months after Willkie became president of Commonwealth and Southern, Franklin Roosevelt asked for a bill which among other things called for the development of the Tennessee River, the production, distribution, and sale of electric power to private corporations, individuals, states, counties, and municipalities. The President's request was granted and became law under the Norris-Rankin Act. From the date of Roosevelt's speech, April 10, 1933, to August, 1939 Willkie, although approving of the principle of the Tennessee Valley Authority, was its most vocal critic. The reason for this was that T.V.A. was to become, in many instances, a competitor with Commonwealth and Southern.

In 1935, the Holding Act was passed. Upon passage of the Act, the Associated Gas and Electric Company ordered its subsidiaries to burn their records. Instead of taking such drastic action, Willkie fought the Act within the traditional American framework. He went to Washington and testified before Congressional committees. As a matter of fact, he spent almost all of 1935 in Washington. His fight against the Holding Company Act was one in which he barred no holds; but, nonetheless, it was in the best tradition of the democratic process.

The Act had a clause which was designed to force the dissolution, after a stipulated interval, of all companies except those that controlled single integrated systems of operating companies. This clause was aimed directly at companies like Commonwealth and Southern. Willkie dubbed this the "death sentence" clause. His testimony before the Congressional committees with respect to the Holding Company Act gave him his first national prominence. It is true that he did not win many of these early battles with the New Deal, but his arguments attracted national attention.

In 1935, Willkie began to use the mass media of communication in order to make others aware of what he considered a life and death struggle. He wrote for *Forbes, Current History, Wharton Review, Public Utilities Fortnightly, Journal of Land and Public Utility Economy,* and the *Magazine of Wall Street.*

Aside from his fights with the New Deal, Willkie was a reformer in the utilities industry proper. He fought against bankers on boards of directors. In fact, Commonwealth and Southern, by 1937, retained only one banker on its board. More important than this, Willkie recognized the necessity of increasing volume and lowering prices. In other words, he believed in the concept that an economic system's basic problems were, first, large-scale production, and second, the distribution of that production to as many people as possible at the lowest possible rate. General Hugh S. Johnson said that Willkie's plan depended on one thing — selling it to the customers. "So he went out to sell it in the way that fits him best — persistence and peddling at every crossroad in his vast sales territory . . . he was unconsciously selling something else — to wit, Wendell Willkie himself — which seems to be no task."

Of course, many of Willkie's ventures were looked upon with disgust by the arch tories of the utilities industry. According to *Fortune* magazine, the conservatives within the industry tried to persuade the people against public ownership by influencing the schools and universities rather than roundabout methods of low rates and progressive selling which Willkie was using. Despite Willkie's progressive businesslike attitude, he had the same basic aim as the conservatives and was not afraid to be candid about it. He did not like to use the words "service to our customers or public service." He felt that this job in a profit-making economy was to work for the stockholders. *Fortune* inquired "whether such stout dogma can steer a sullen and suspect old-guard industry remains to be seen."

In reviewing Willkie's battles with the New Deal, it is clear that his primary attack was not against government ownership as such. He did not believe in government ownership, but he said if the people wanted it they should have it. His real fight was against unlimited invasion on the part of government. As the government's competitor, he never knew when it would cut its rates or how far it would extend its lines. He felt that it should choose an area, and limit its activities to it. Government should buy already existing properties, rather than merely destroying them with irresistible competition. Willkie was asking nothing unreasonable. Finally, in 1939, he did sell to the government the Commonwealth and Southern properties that had been in competition with T.V.A. In completing this sale he won a partial victory in that he received the price that he had asked for the properties.

Willkie as a leader of the utilities industry was neither a reticent banker nor an inarticulate engineer, but a lawyer, and a lawyer both willing and able to talk. Furthermore, he described himself as a liberal and had a pretty fair title to the description.

Willkie, by 1937, began to find a larger market for his ideas. In August of that year he wrote an article for *Atlantic Monthly,* "Political Power." In this he pointed out the dangers of the unlimited exercise of political power. He cautioned against any group being permitted to control the actions of men. Further, Willkie argued that there should be a proper balance of power between the various major groups in the country.

On January 6, 1938, Willkie debated with the Administration's spokesman, Robert Jackson, on the subject, "How Can Business and Government Work Together?" His plea in this appearance was for an Administration that did not hate business, rather one that could work with business for the benefit of the whole country. The debate ended in a clear Willkie victory. It was the last time that a Democratic national leader dared to challenge Willkie until Harold Ickes came forward in April of 1940. Willkie appeared on the *New York Herald Tribune* Forum in October of 1938, where once again he was able to reach a large audience. From the titles of the magazine articles that he continued to write, and the publications in which they appeared, one can see that he was not confining himself to the issues which would be of particular interest to a utilities executive: "Idle Men — Idle Money," "With Malice Toward None," and "The Court Is Now His," appeared in *The Saturday Evening Post;* "Brace Up America," was published in *Atlantic Monthly.*

Any change, however, that took place in Willkie was slow and subtle. He spent most of his time in Washington occupying a suite at the Mayflower Hotel observing government as it works. He was drinking and talking with the Washington correspondents who were later to be of invaluable service to him. It is probably accurate to say that no other candidate for President has ever known Washington so well without ever having held an elective or appointed federal job. Willkie was a high-class lobbyist. Harold Laski saw Willkie as "a vigorous personality, with fire and courage, and the kind of easy charm Americans like." It is no wonder that such a man as this should be mentioned as a presidential prospect.

Mary E. Dillon, a Willkie biographer, writes of an exchange that took place between A. C. Oliphant and Willkie in the spring of 1939. Oliphant told Willkie that "with all the publicity you have been receiving you had better be careful or you will suddenly find yourself a candidate for President." Willkie's reply was that "they will never drag me into something like that." But Willkie was to be persuaded — not a particularly hard job — to seek the Republican nomination.

On February 23, 1939, Arthur Krock first mentioned Willkie as a possible candidate. His suggestion was quickly taken up by others. Raymond Moley, a month later, labelled Willkie as an excellent man for President because he had demonstrated the ability "to think, speak, and act effectively." The consensus of the news analysts was that Willkie was brilliant, experienced, and well schooled in public affairs. Hugh Johnson, during April, mentioned Willkie as a man who could take over Roosevelt's job. A reporter who was covering Johnson's speech called Willkie. Willkie's reply to the reporter's question as to whether he would like the job was typical of the statements that the public liked. "If the government keeps taking away my business at its recent rate, I'll soon be looking for a job. Johnson's offer is the best that I have had yet."

As the presidential talk increased, Arthur Krock offered some advice on the "care and feeding of dark horses." He noted that Willkie was not taking the prospect seriously and that this was an important factor in the delicate science of conditioning. Willkie might not have been taking the talk seriously, but he was taking other things seriously; to wit, his intellectual integrity. In a personal letter to Krock he said that he would refuse the nomination of a major party if the party did not draft a platform that he could respect. He added: "Now, please understand me — I have no illusions that any party is going to nominate me."

Willkie's preservation of intellectual integrity was, no doubt, one of the things which made the people realize that he was no ordinary man. Willkie, for all practical purposes, was following the formula laid down by Lord Bryce many years before, when he said: "I doubt if there be any country [other than the U.S.] where a really confident man, confident in his own strength and adding the charm of a striking personality to the gift of popular eloquence, would find an easier path to fame and power, and could exert more influence over the minds and emotions of the multitudes. Such a man speaking to the people with independence of conscious strength, would find himself appreciated and respected." By late 1939 Willkie was finding himself "appreciated and respected."

Willkie's abiding faith in his early years was in the ideals and memories of Woodrow Wilson. He had grown up as a Democrat and had continued as one until late 1938. Moreover, he had willingly supported much of the New Deal. In international politics he was a firm believer in the League of Nations and had backed Newton D. Baker for the Democratic presidential nomination because of this belief. In 1938, after his many struggles with the New Deal, he had no concrete political goals. While speaking before the *New York Herald Tribune* Forum in 1938 he referred directly to the Democratic party, "of which, incidentally I am a member." In this same speech he went on to say that the Administration had been right in many of the social and economic reforms that it had put into effect. He felt that "industrial and social needs have outgrown regulation by states."

Despite his adherence to much of the New Deal, he began to tour the country speaking his mind. At Wooster College in late January of 1940 he told the audience that he was not running for President. "I couldn't go out and seek delegates and make two-sided statements." He spoke frankly, saying the things that people wanted to hear, and things that they had been hoping someone would say, the things that they had been thinking. His speeches and articles were clearly reasoned and restrained presentations which just happened to hit an unsounded key-note in the thinking of millions of people. In them there was nothing highbrow and nothing hateful. They revealed a big Hoosier talking sense in barnyard but engaging language.

What was Willkie saying that aroused public interest? In the first place he disregarded the old cliches and slogans. True, he was, in many cases, merely re-stating traditional American thinking, but there was more to it than that. Willkie was espousing a new doctrine of liberalism — one which combined the best of the philosophy that "the business of America is business" and the philosophy of the New Deal. He was an unusual mixture of critic of the age and at the same time spokesman for it.

Willkie felt that the common denominator for all those of a liberal faith was the desire to make men free. "It is not," he said, "the purpose of the liberal to prevent the limitations of poverty, insecurity, and weakness of freedom." He believed that the liberal "is one who prefers, as Newton Baker once stated it, 'to be poor if necessary, but in any case free'." More specifically Willkie was offering a philosophy which would grant no absolute power to any group. He believed in curbing the power of "big money," "big government," and "big labor." He was for economic and social reforms so long as they did not destroy the freedom which they were attempting to create. This was a new type of appeal. Here was a man ready to concede a point to his enemies, but not all points.

As the campaign proceeded and Willkie's utterances on domestic policy became more specific, his saying what the people were thinking became more pronounced. Oren Root says that Willkie was shrewd in knowing just what to say. He sensed that the country was tired of the run-of-the-mill politician and that the American public was more interested in ideas. His famous "We, the People" article which appeared in the April 1940 issue of *Fortune,* was predicated on that assumption. Willkie was, in effect, becoming a symbol of hope to many for whom the New Deal had been a failure.

Willkie was a big business man who had been in constant conflict with the federal government. He could tell the people, as he did at Wooster College, that the people who thought business was something apart from their lives were wrong. "It is a part of our life." Further, he said that those who were not in business could not say that the restrictions placed on business would not affect them. In his speeches there was no aversion to pointing out the abuses of both government and business. He said, jokingly, that we will come upon men doing bad. But he added, "It is hardly a good practice to kill the patient in order to prevent a recurrence of the disease." Willkie could not understand those opposed to the Administration who thought that they had to be 100 per cent against it. His hope was that "when election time rolls around the voter will not be forced to make a choice between two half-rotten apples."

Willkie returned to this theme frequently. In an article, "What I Would Do as President," in *Barron's* he pointed out that there had been "malefactors of great wealth, . . . and of small wealth, and . . . labor leaders who had betrayed their trusts." He was equally harsh with government saying that "we want no more men in high office to act as provocative agents of class warfare." He said that the hope that the New Deal meant a truly liberal government was gone. It had an opportunity, "certainly no liberal movement ever had a greater."

In his last written plea — appropriately entitled "Five Minutes to Midnight" — prior to the convention, he stressed the fact that our economic system needed to recover. We had had reforms but not recovery. "The great reforms which the people demanded in the early thirties have now been accomplished." Despite these reforms, government still looked upon business as the enemy. In clear language he called for "a completely different attitude on the part of the government toward business. We want no more epithets. We want no more attacks on the men who make money. We want more men who make money." This article and other articles and speeches served to express Willkie's position. Other men might have been called presumptuous for using "we." But Willkie's use of the first person plural was accepted, because he had been speaking as a representative of "We, the People."

Aside from the position Willkie took on government and business there were other issues upon which he took a stand. The problem of agriculture was one that was critical. He felt that no one had worked out an adequate solution to the problem. He approved of the principle of conservation, but pointed out the policy had been used to destroy foodstuffs. The two things which would help agriculture, according to Willkie, were business recovery and reciprocal trade treaties. He never advised stopping the Roosevelt program until a better one was offered.

The tax program that Willkie advocated was at variance with the Roosevelt one. His plan was to increase inheritance taxes, give the same weight to losses in capital gains tax as was given to gains, keep the tax on large incomes within proper limits, impose a tax on state and other government securities. Along with the revision of the tax program he called for a balanced budget, but unlike the other Republican aspirants he did not see how this could be done in a year or even two. The deficit, however, could be reduced. He said that the New Deal had not even made the first step in the right direction.

Willkie maintained a sense of humor in all of his speeches. In Topeka, Kansas, he announced that he was the "cockiest fellow that you ever saw." If the people did not want to vote for him, he advised them to go jump in a lake. All during the campaign he had indicated his willingness to run against Roosevelt. Instead of denouncing the President he looked forward to debating with him. "I would," he stated, "like to go on the stump and debate with the President the question of whether the job I did in utilities was not far better than the job he has done in the past seven years."

In speaking out on domestic issues, Willkie was filling a role. His own split reaction to the Roosevelt reforms, over the preceding six years, qualified him to play the part of frustrated business man, both for business and the Republican party. He did not so much create the role as fill it. Once his fame began to grow he could not meet the demands to speak which various groups placed upon him. Disclaiming a desire for the nomination at first and later saying that he was willing to accept it only on his terms was not enough to keep enthusiastic men from advocating his nomination. It was more or less assumed that Willkie was a Republican. His boom appears to have grown just like Topsy. Whenever anyone would ask one of his supporters which nomination Willkie was seeking the reply was "the Republican, naturally, he is against Roosevelt."

Colonel Breckenridge, an independent Democrat who had run in four primaries against Roosevelt in 1936, said that "as a light horse in the dark, Willkie stands in contrast with the other candidates." Willkie had every right to the "light horse" label in the sense that his supporters were not professional politicians who usually maneuver the "dark horse" into position.

Oren Root, grandnephew of Elihu Root, was the first full time Willkie amateur. Root heard Willkie speak at Princeton in April of 1940. He was surprised at what he heard and decided that Willkie was the man for the Republican nomination. Young Root had supported LaGuardia in his 1937 campaign for mayor of New York City and Thomas Dewey for governor of New York in 1938. He took a leave of absence from the Wall Street law firm of Davis, Polk, Wardwell, Gardiner, Reed, and Root to send out Willkie-for-President declarations to college graduates. The first petitions were mailed on April 9, 1940. The New York lawyer did not know Willkie at this time and did not ask his consent to send the declarations. On April 22, Root opened an office in New York and by April 30 he was able to say that at least 200,000 people had signed the declarations.

Root was joined in this venture of championing the candidacy of Willkie by Russell Davenport who had been managing editor of *Fortune*. Davenport joined the Willkie crusade because he believed that the utilities executive stood for certain principles "more clearly and more forcibly than any other candidate." Davenport had met Willkie while the latter was working on an article for *Fortune*. Davenport's job was to integrate the efforts of his friend Root and the Volunteer Mailing Committee for Distribution of Willkie's speeches. Robert L. Johnson, president of Robert L. Johnson Magazines, assisted Davenport in this integrative work.

Frank Altschul, a member of Lazard Frères Company, investment bankers, and a past chairman of the Republican Finance Committee, became attracted to Willkie when he heard Willkie debate Robert Jackson in 1938. Altschul was influential in getting Senator Styles Bridges to support Willkie. Bridges, upon completion of a nationwide tour, talked with Altschul and told him that there was a definite spirit for Willkie; furthermore, Bridges promised that he would aid Willkie in the convention.

Another early Willkie advocate was Samuel Pryor, Connecticut Republican National Committeeman. Pryor invited Willkie to speak at the two-hundredth anniversary of the founding of the Christ Church in Greenwich, Connecticut. Early in 1940 the *New York Sun* published a story that Willkie was a Republican. Pryor, who was impressed with the Greenwich speech, rushed to Willkie's office and got him to issue a press release substantiating the *Sun's* story.

One of the most important strategists in the Willkie camp was Charlton MacVeagh, litterateur and industrialist. MacVeagh wrote all the early campaign literature and most of Willkie's speeches. He became the contact between the amateurs and the professional politicians who labored for Willkie. Harold E. Talbott, Wall Street capitalist and polo-playing sportsman, was another wealthy member of the original team who worked with the Associated Willkie Clubs, which had risen spontaneously. Congressman Bruce Barton of New York and Governor William Vanderbilt of Rhode Island were early Willkie advocates among the politicians proper.

Davenport, Root, Altschul, Bridges, Pryor, Johnson, Talbott, MacVeagh, Barton, and Vanderbilt, the uninvited, formed the group which gave Willkie his only organized pre-convention support. There was no money except Willkie's and that was used to pay travelling expenses and the salaries of a couple of research girls. However, there was no great need for money or organized support as such since the other candidates had such a head start on Willkie. Willkie and his supporters realized that their only hope of capturing the nomination was to have the convention become dissatisfied with the other candidates and select Willkie as the best compromise in sight. Some men grow coy and prim when overtaken by a nationwide compliment and the possibility of a major party nomination, but this was not the case with Willkie. He did not propose to waste any time running for the nomination and that was all there was to it. Willkie told the others to go to it if they wished. An overt attempt by Willkie to win delegates would have been a nice spectacle but would not have aided Willkie.

Although not waging battle for delegates, Willkie did try to win public support. His appearance on the radio show "Information Please," April 9, 1940, was one of the most astute political moves that he made. No doubt, the professional wits were ready to slaughter the guest expert. Instead, he ran away with the program, and a national audience, most of whom had never heard of Commonwealth and Southern, now knew who Willkie was and liked him. Willkie answered more questions than the encyclopedic wit, John Kieran. *United States News* claimed that the appearance was not planned as a publicity stunt, but it was, in effect, the best single piece of publicity that any candidate received.

The Willkie-Ickes debate was one of the highlights of the campaign. The debate took place before the Press Club in Washington in April. Ickes refused to speak first although he was defending the proposition that the President should seek a third term. Willkie in his first speech argued that the President should not run because there were too many good men available, one being Harold Ickes. When Ickes arose to speak, he recited some doggerel poetry. In rebuttal Willkie said, "Mr. Ickes will have to write better poetry than that if he wants my vote." For the most part the debate was a humorous exchange and contained none of the bitter denunciations of the President that the other candidates had used.

In May, Willkie accepted a speaking engagement in Minneapolis. The speech was broadcast and Willkie read a very mediocre prepared speech. At the completion of the radio address Willkie threw the unstapled manuscript into the air and said: "Some damn fool told me I had to read a speech to you. Now, let me tell you what I really think." The audience reaction was so favorable that he tried the same approach in Des Moines, Iowa.

It was at this Minneapolis speech that Willkie began to think that he could win the nomination. "I think the first time I took it [the possibility of receiving the nomination] seriously was on May 11 . . . Because that was the day on which I was invited to speak before the Minnesota Republicans. That was after my debate with the well-known gladiator, Harold Ickes." In fact, the Minnesota appearance was the first one that Willkie made before a Republican organization.

The popularity that Willkie achieved was not wholly spontaneous. Although no organized group of public opinion specialists was working for Willkie, he had the influential support of a group of independent business and advertising executives who did all they could to mold public opinion favorably to Willkie. William H. Harmon, vice-president of the Baldwin Locomotive Works, describes the intent of one of the independent groups. "I," Harmon stated, "regard this as a serious religious movement and we are trying to get it on a revival basis."

Fred Smith, of Selvage and Smith advertising agency and publicity director of Congressman Bruce Barton's campaign, did Willkie's newspaper work. Smith, as he had done with Barton, saw to it that pictures of Willkie in humble settings were given currency. *Tide,* the magazine of business and advertising, said that Smith circulated a biography of Willkie's tumultuous youth. The biography contained a vow of Samuel Insull, public utilities magnate, that he would destroy Willkie, and Willkie's statement that Wall Street was "a bunch of jugglers."

Among the advertising experts who helped Willkie were Harry Schackleford, advertising manager of Johns Manville; the famed publicity man Steve Hannegan; Ned Stevens, counsellor on radio advertising; Edgar Queeny of Monsanto Chemical Corporation; Stanley Resor and J. Walter Thompson, San Francisco advertising executives; John Young who started a chain letter which allegedly reached ninety-three million people; and A. P. Giannini, founder of the Bank of America, a California banker who had aided the Roosevelt campaign of 1936. This aid by the subtle specialists in public relations merely complemented the wise course Willkie chose for himself.

The rising Willkie fortunes during April, 1940, began to attract more attention than the favorite sons or professionals. But much had to be done in May to pave the way for Willkie's nomination in June. Dr. George Gallup, the public opinion analyst, said that Willkie's rise was an interesting study in presidential booms. As late as March, a Gallup survey found Willkie named by only a few Republicans. Then, with no effort on Willkie's part, a boom started overnight. The boom began in the financial and professional districts of New York and swung out to the business communities of the Eastern seaboard and most of the larger metropolitan areas of the West; then it penetrated the rural areas.

By convention time there were seven hundred Willkie-for-President Clubs. This tremendous popularity rise was partly a result of the newspaper men who were for Willkie. The primary backing from this element came from the Cowles brothers of the *Des Moines Register and Tribune* and the *Minneapolis Star-Journal.* The columnists who were favorable to Willkie included Ray Clapper, Mark Sullivan, Walter Lippman, Westbrook Pegler, Hugh Johnson and Frank Kent. By the middle of June, the powerful Scripps-Howard chain and the *Philadelphia Evening Ledger* came out for Willkie. Kenneth Simpson and other Dewey foes helped call the attention of the newspapers to Willkie's dramatic and personable qualities.

Willkie's popularity with newspapermen, for the most part, was of long standing and needed little bolstering from other sources. He called many of them by their first names, drank with them, and talked with them in a candid manner. Reporters, during the T.V.A. fight, asked Willkie this standard question: "What are you going to Washington for, Mr. Willkie?" Willkie's reply was: "Oh, to see that my contempt for the New Deal remains founded on familiarity."

There was another reason why the preponderant mass of daily and weekly journals was for Willkie. Support for him was dictated by business considerations — prosperity and influence were to be had by building up Willkie. There is still another reason advanced for newspaper and magazine support. This was that a certain sense for news told editors that the Republican leaders were suffering from the fidgets, and that once in two or three blue moons a dark horse wins.

The unearned increment of politics is an important factor in winning group support. Undoubtedly, the statement of William Green, president of the American Federation of Labor, helped Willkie to receive his share of the unearned increment of politics. Green said that "cooperative relationships prevail" between the Georgia subsidiary of Commonwealth and Southern and the American Federation of Labor's local union. Green's announcement was one which helped quell the talk that Willkie as a big businessman was naturally anti-labor. In fact, the Green statement probably induced many laborers to support Willkie for the nomination.

There were many points in Willkie's favor. He had taken a middle-of-the-road stand with respect to the New Deal. He was a new kind of personality — a big, shaggy, outspoken, and energetic utilities leader. His candidacy had gained the support of many enthusiastic amateurs. In reality, however, these factors only served to catch the national eye and ear. It was the war in Europe which gave Willkie the edge over the other candidates.

Willkie had been a long time advocate of reciprocal trade agreements. In his "We, the People" article he had stated that to erase tariffs immediately would be ruinous. He said that the present Secretary of State, Cordull Hull, who is a "wise and temperate man, recognized this, and so he adopted reciprocal agreements." Willkie thought that this policy was simple and in accord with common sense. "What could be better qualified to benefit us, the people, as a whole?" Further, he did not have much faith in the figures cited by the Republicans to show how harmful the agreements had been. To the people this plea for reciprocal trade seemed to be logical.

The German invasion of the Scandinavian countries early in April gave Willkie an opportunity to extend his international cooperation attitude. He had written in March that the "world is closely knit . . . so dependent upon each other, that it is not realistic to make domestic policies without considering their relationship to foreign affairs." Willkie, as the war in Europe grew worse, proclaimed that we had a vital interest in the continuance of the British and French way of life. The *New York Times* praised Willkie for his candor. Of course, he did not advocate armed intervention, but he did take a position that the other Republican candidates considered dangerous. "The most effective way," he said, "of keeping out of this war will be by helping the democracies in every way possible." This stand won the support of many eastern seaboard Republicans. On the other hand, it was considered too aggressive by many other Republicans.

Willkie toured the Middlewest in the middle of May and continued his pro-ally pronouncements. James Hagerty reported that the so-called isolationist belt had changed its traditional point of view if the audience reaction to Willkie's speeches was an adequate indicator. Back in New York after his midwestern swing, Willkie said that the man who felt the events in Europe were of no consequence to us was a "blind, foolish and silly man."

Akron, Ohio's American Legion Post, was the setting for Willkie's most extreme pre-convention statement on the foreign situation. "It is clear that England and France constitute our first line of defense against Hitler. If anybody is going to stop Hitler from further aggression, they are the ones who will do it. Just putting it in the most selfish light, if Britain and France lick Hitler now, we may be saved billions of dollars . . . It must, therefore, be to our advantage to help them in every way we can, short of declaring war." In taking this position Willkie was following his own advice, for he had often criticized people who did not say what they thought. Men were, according to him, reluctant to speak their minds because they feared the loss of support from this or that group. This was, in essence, the curse of democracy. "And this fear has altogether perverted the process of democracy and sapped its strength." Willkie, unhampered by this fear, had been at one time far in advance of public opinion. By late May and early June while the Dunkerque evacuation was taking place, public opinion had begun to converge with the Willkie stand.

When Italy declared war on France and England Franklin Roosevelt made his most belligerent statement to that date. "On this tenth day of June, 1940, the hand that held the dagger has stuck it into the back of its neighbor." The press backing of Roosevelt was almost unanimous. The *New York Times* said that "few Italians believe that they will see the war to a finish without having America against them." This, then, was another incident to prove the validity of Willkie's position.

In the meantime Dewey, with bravado, was fumbling with the topic of foreign affairs, and Taft appeared to be running to the wrong goal post. On the other hand, Willkie had seized the ball. William Allen White observed: "Willkie seems to be the only candidate who would definitely and consciously wipe out any discussion of the foreign question beyond armament in the Republican platform. The foreign question will dominate the Republican convention and probably the foreign issue will name the Republican candidate." White, by implication, was predicting the eventual nomination of Willkie.

Despite the growing feeling that Willkie would be nominated, serious obstacles stood in his way. Perhaps the greatest was the fact that Willkie had been a Democrat until 1938. In 1935, Willkie was a member of the New York City Democratic Committee which included James Farley, Bernard Baruch and Frank Walker. Willkie was a dues paying member of this committee until 1936. This was a drawback because the Republicans had not nominated a party deviate in their history. Willkie's Democratic affiliation was continuously mentioned. David Ingalls, Taft's campaign manager, made a statement typical of those being made when he argued that the party should nominate a Republican.

Willkie, as a captain of the utilities industry, was in the worst kind of big business, private electric power, which had been guilty of many abuses. There were those who felt that no convention composed of politicians would venture to nominate a buisnessman regardless of his abilities. Willkie, unlike Taft, Dewey, and Vandenberg, had never held public office. This was another factor that disturbed the politicians, not because they had any lofty concern about his executive abilities, but because they were fearful about Willkie as a political administrator, as a dispenser of jobs and favors, as a sympathetic patron of the party workers. Aside from the patronage worries, there was the fact that Willkie had never proved that he could win votes — a *sine qua non* of American politics.

Willkie's unknown quality as a vote-getter, however, was modified by his rapid improvement in the public opinion polls. In fact, his rapid rise in popularity became something of a disadvantage. The Gallup Poll shows the Willkie rise as follows:

	May 8 PER CENT	May 17 PER CENT	May 31 PER CENT	June 12 PER CENT	June 21 PER CENT
Dewey	67	62	56	52	31
Taft	12	14	16	13	5
Vandenberg	14	13	12	12	5
Willkie	3	5	10	17	29
Hoover	2	2	2	2	4
Others	2	4	4	4	2
Undecided	–	–	–	–	24

This sudden upsurge gave the appearance of a popular bandwagon, even while the politicians were doubtful that Willkie was the man for the nomination. *United States News* reported that all the candidates were in the stop-Willkie camp prior to the convention, with the exception of Senator Bridges. Others who were opposed to Willkie's nomination included: Herbert Hoover, Jim Watson, former senator from Indiana; Senators David Reed and Joseph Grundy of Pennsylvania.

Willkie probably was aware of these handicaps, but nonetheless on June 12 he said: "I think the nomination for President is going to come quickly. . . . The nomination will be made on the sixth or seventh ballot. . . . My supporters say that I will be nominated and I think that I should be." He was an apt predictor, but at the time he was so confident, his delegate strength was almost nonexistent. However, the forces and conditions were converging. It took a Philadelphia Miracle to make them coalesce.

Hungerford in the Pittsburgh Post-Gazette

"How The Old Place Has Changed"

"WE WANT WILLKIE"

Amid the open, raucous, mad palaver of those vast public powwows reverberating across the states over radio, by telephone and telegraph wires, runs an undercurrent of intrigue. The convention intrigue is not influenced by the noise of shouting captains. But all of these elements of democratic expression—blaring bands, conspiracies, calithumpian clowning and secret omens—write in some strange, weird way the results.

One could hardly deny the validity of William Allen White's statement. National conventions are in some respects national circuses. But they also are engaged in serious business. The national conventions give us a panoramic view of the democratic process as it manifests itself at a critical point. The presidential nominating convention dates from the collapse of the caucus and the Anti-Mason convention of 1831. It has now become part and parcel of our life. It is extra-legal and extra-constitutional, just like political parties. In 1940 this great democratic invention was the instrument through which a divided and pessimistic party made one of the most important selections in its history.

The dates for the two major conventions were decided early in February. Republican National Chairman John Hamilton, in announcing that the Republican convention would be held in Philadelphia beginning June 24, was full of bravado when he challenged the Democrats to nominate Roosevelt. "We would," he said, "have a clear cut issue, and once and for all we would have a showdown on the New Deal, Franklin Roosevelt, and the third term — then we would finish all three." The Democrats, meeting after the Republicans, picked their site and date — Chicago, July 15. The date of the Democratic convention was the latest since 1864. This, however, is not startling when one considers the time and troubles that the nation faced.

Events had been fast moving since John Hamilton issued his challenge to the Democrats. On the eve of their convention the Republicans could not be sure of whom the Democrats would nominate or what the Democratic platform would be. On the other hand, no Republican aspirant was assured of his party's nomination and a bitter battle was being waged over the Republican platform. Uncertainty and suspense were in the Philadelphia political air.

Marquis Childs described the Philadelphia scene: "The station wagon set had come down from New York for the big show. The town was gay with the right hats. There were good parties all over the place." The first delegation to arrive was the Texans, who reported that there was "plenty of whiskey on the train but not a six-shooter in the crowd." In many respects these two groups represent the two main elements at the Republican convention of 1940 — the station wagon set or the political amateurs, and the fun-loving political convention old-time professionals.

The realization that there could not be a repeat performance of 1936 was one of the convention undercurrents. As the convention assembled, it appeared that the nominee would be selected by an open and free convention. There would not be another first ballot Landon. The likelihood of deals and coalitions, such as had affected nominations in the past, was less than at any time. There were several factors which account for this attitude. First, the Republicans had been out of power so long that the practical reins of leadership — patronage — were missing. Second, the times were confused and the delegates could not escape this. They realized that there were no easy answers and that the professionals did not have a monopoly on the right course of action.

An outward manifestation of the un-bossed convention was the fact that all of the major candidates were in attendance for the first time since 1920. They were forced to go in order to make a direct appeal to the delegates. Another indication of the uncertain nature of the convention was that there were many uninstructed and "favorite son" delegations. Only two primaries, Nebraska and Wisconsin, had been battlefields for the aspirants. This lack of unanimity resulted from the Republicans not having a clear choice prior to the convention.

In light of these circumstances it was difficult to estimate just how much delegate strength each candidate would have. Nonetheless, there were predictions. It was generally agreed that Dewey would have about 370, Taft 250, Vandenberg 100, Willkie 100, and "favorite sons" 180.

Dewey was admitted to be the front runner. He expected the convention to nominate him on the first or second ballot. One observer said that he had never seen such self-confidence since the evening he had spent at Tony Galento's. But somehow Dewey lost his pre-convention color. Dewey and his supporters' activities took on a drab tinge upon arrival in Philadelphia. In part, this resulted from their concentrating on practical politics — holding pledges, shopping for votes, and avoiding the Willkie whirlwind. This resort to practical politics was partly due to the feeling that if Dewey were to be nominated it would to be on an early ballot. The notion of Dewey's need for a quick kill had been expressed as early as May 6.

Analysts, prior to the convention, felt that if Dewey failed to get the nomination, Senator Taft would be given a chance. This idea was based on Taft's support from the professional politicians. In essence, it meant that Dewey, despite his youth and inexperience, was the first choice of the party regulars as a vote-getter. Further, if the convention should fail to give Dewey the nomination, the man of stability and party regularity, Senator Taft, would get an opportunity. But Taft, like Dewey, was a colorless convention figure. He was not a colorful figure in any surrounding and the misty political weather of a convention had not changed him.

Senator Vandenberg, in view of his primary defeats and refusal to campaign, was practically out of the running. He was shrouded by the convention atmosphere. However, there still existed the possibility that he might be the candidate if there was a deadlock.

The big question mark was Willkie. Willkie had few delegate pledges, but he appeared to be the only candidate that was gaining. This is an important advantage in politics. Political horse races are not won in the first few furlongs, not even on the last turn, but in the home stretch. It was the home stretch upon which Willkie was counting. His supporters were enthusiastic and presented a fifth column menace to other candidates. In fact, the national committeemen were disillusioned to find their delegates slipping off to the Willkie headquarters for conferences instead of asking them how to vote.

Much to the delight of his supporters, Willkie was continuing his pre-convention antics. He set out to woo the delegates just as he had the pre-convention audiences. Willkie saved himself a lot of time by going without sleep. He lived on six packs of cigarettes a day and coffee. For the first time the politicians were getting a look at Willkie. He was showing them the actions about which they had been reading. He was providing the convention with much needed color, and saving it from total drabness. Willkie was still a novelty, a sparkling political prism and a thrilling entertainment. He was a sight to behold as he raced through the lobbies, heaving his burly person in and out of taxicabs and projecting his individual dynamism into speeches to the delegates.

As Willkie was winning new supporters, the "stop Willkie" movement gained adherents. A group of forty Congressmen from twenty states met and issued a statement aimed at Willkie. The statement, in part, said: "The Republican party will win in November if it selects from its ranks a leader with a past record consistently supporting Republican policies and whose recognized position and recent pronouncements are a guarantee to the American people that he will not lead the nation into a foreign war." This statement was sent to all the delegates. There was little doubt that these Congressional leaders were fearful lest the party should nominate a man like Willkie who was committed to all-out aid to the Allies.

The Republican Congressional leaders' announcement was made in the face of the gravest crisis in the European war. One week before the convention opened the French had asked Germany for peace. On June 22, the French-German armistice was signed. And on the day that the convention assembled the terms of the peace were learned. These developments had a tremendous effect on the entire convention and particularly upon the Resolutions Committee which had been called into session one week before the convention opened. The Committee had written all the planks except the foreign policy one by June 22. The fall of France forced the Committee to reconsider its stand on foreign affairs and thereby prolonged the final report on the platform until the second day of the convention. The battle that was being waged within the Committee was between the Dewey-Taft isolationists and the internationalists. Herbert K. Hyde, a Dewey supporter and an isolationist, was selected as chairman of the platform committee. The sub-committee on foreign affairs was headed by Alf Landon who by this time was for all aid to the Allies short of war.

The Resolutions Committee's problem was further complicated when Roosevelt, two days before the convention opened, appointed Henry Stimson and Colonel Knox to his cabinet. These appointments were especially irritating to the Republicans since Knox had been their Vice-Presidential candidate in 1936 and Stimson had served in the cabinets of two Republican Presidents. When the convention received news of this sudden move, John Hamilton proceeded to read the two "traitors" out of the party. "As members," stated Hamilton, "of the President's cabinet, they owe their allegiance to the President and hereafter will speak and act in that capacity."

Dewey said that Roosevelt's action meant a "direct step towards war." Taft concluded that the "Democratic party is becoming a war party." Willkie, on the other hand, took a calmer view of the situation and said that "each conscientious individual had to determine such things according to the dictates of his own conscience." Regardless of the President's intention he turned the spotlight directly on the Republican problem and the battle that was being waged in the Resolutions Committee. It had the effect, according to some Republicans, of sabotaging the convention.

There were other signs of the struggle that was taking place over the foreign policy plank. Within the Republican ranks there existed two equally vocal organizations — "The Committee to Defend America by Aiding the Allies" and "The National Committee to Keep America Out of War." The former group was not exclusively Republican, but the force behind it was William Allen White, the Emporia, Kansas editor. The latter group was headed by Congressmen Hamilton Fish and Harold Knutson. This committee bought full page advertisements in the various eastern newspapers. The plea of the advertisements was for the people to wire the Republican delegates and ask for an anti-war plank. The White Committee was employing the same methods, but they were asking for aid to the Allies short of war.

On the second day of the convention, after repeated delays, the Resolutions Committee despite all the pressure that had been placed on it was able to present an acceptable foreign policy plank. The statement contained two main points. The first charged that Franklin Roosevelt was guilty of the lack of preparedness and that this gave rise to the possibility of American involvement in the war. The second was advocacy of aid to the Allies. The complete statement of this point follows: "We favor the extension to all peoples fighting for liberty, or whose liberty is threatened, of such aid as shall not be in violation of international law or inconsistent with the requirements of our own national defense." Two isolationists, Hamilton Fish and C. Wayland "Curly" Brooks, and one internationalist, Henry Cabot Lodge, Jr., indicated their approval of the plank. The isolationists saw the pronouncement as being anti-war while Lodge believed that the Republicans had recognized and accepted international responsibility.

The language of the Resolutions Committee was far more noncommittal on the international question than the language Willkie had been using during his campaign. The wording was such that a Republican Presidential candidate could advocate as much or as little aid to the Allies as he deemed adequate. It was a two-sided statement, but it did serve to cement, for public purposes, the split in the party which had taken place between the isolationists and the internationalists. More important, perhaps, is that the leaders and aspirants were satisfied with the stand.

Aside from the Resolutions Committee, the activities of only one other convention committee, the Committee on Arrangements, created a controversy. Samuel Pryor, an early Willkie enthusiast, had replaced Ralph E. Williams of Oregon as chairman of the Committee on Arrangements when the latter died. Pryor had been chairman of the subcommittee on tickets. This seems to be an innocent enough shift, but it had interesting implications. During the course of the convention Colonel Creager, Taft's floor leader, charged Pryor with having issued special tickets to Willkie backers. "You," Creager told Pryor, "issued them for the candidacy of your man Willkie. You have perpetuated an outrage on the Republican Party and dealt unfairly with the other candidates . . . No other candidate knew of the issuance of these tickets." An investigation of this charge was made by the Assistant Sergeant-at-Arms, Sam S. Lewis. Lewis found that the Committee on Arrangements, at Pryor's instigation, had issued thousands of tickets which deviated from the original ticket. The special tickets were as follows:

REPUBLICAN NATIONAL CONVENTION
June, 1940
SPECIAL ADMISSION
Entrance 23

This was a highly irregular move on Pryor's part. On Walter Cronkite's television show, "The Twentieth Century," December 16, 1961, Pryor recalled this incident and glossed over it by saying that tickets were distributed to those outside the convention hall who wanted in on a first come, first served basis. According to Pryor, "nine out of ten" of these people were Willkie supporters so in reality there was no need to stack the galleries.

There is little doubt that these tickets added to the already friendly Willkie galleries. In fact, at the very first session of the convention, a group in one of the balconies shouted, "We Want Willkie," and created the first demonstration in the convention hall. Whether the galleries ever are a factor in nominating a President is open to question. However, Pryor's indiscretion indicates that Willkie and his supporters were playing to the people, hoping that popular demand would help win the nomination.

From the time that Willkie arrived in Philadelphia his activities and those of his advocates were attempts to create the impression that Willkie was the people's choice. One of the men who worked for Willkie called the campaign a masterpiece of disorganization. The campaign was from Wall Street to Main Street, men and women wrote chain letters, sent telegrams, circulated petitions, wore and gave away Willkie buttons with a minimum of direction.

Willkie's play for public opinion was obvious in almost everything he did. Shortly after entering the City of Brotherly Love, Willkie, while walking down the street, was collared by W. C. Tooze, Chairman of the Oregon delegation. Tooze asked Willkie if he favored reciprocal trade agreements. Willkie said that he favored the principle. Tooze began to walk away saying that Willkie had evaded the issue. Thereupon, Willkie grabbed Tooze by the shirt and the following exchange took place. "I'll answer any questions," said Willkie. "I'm for the principle of reciprocal tariffs, a policy advocated by Republican Presidents such as Garfield, McKinley, and Taft." Tooze then asked, "Do you favor aid to the Allies?" Willkie replied, "I favor all possible aid to the Allies without war." "Doesn't that mean war?" some observers asked. "That's a matter of opinion," was Willkie's answer. This was typical of the way in which the "Immortal Amateur" operated during the convention. In effect, he held a perpetual press conference.

From an organizational standpoint, the most amazing situation was the fact that Willkie did not have a board of strategy until the second day of the convention. And had it not been for Arthur Krock and Turner Catledge there is a possibility that Willkie would never have realized the importance of such a group. Mary E. Dillon says that on June 22 at about one o'clock in the morning Willkie met Krock and Catledge going into the Chancellor Hall Apartments. Willkie invited them up to his room for a drink, and according to Dillon the following took place: "The men mixed iceless drinks and began to talk. Krock asked the usual questions as to how everything was going. Naïvely, Willkie replied that everything was going fine. . . . But to the direct question as to the choice of floor leaders, Willkie looked blank. Did he need a floor leader? What was such a person supposed to do?" At this point Catledge and Krock began explaining the functions and necessity of floor leaders.

Krock wrote on Monday, June 24, that the lone professional supporting Willkie was Indiana Congressman Charles Halleck. In the light of his conversation with Willkie on the twenty-second of June, Krock reported that the Willkie camp was still looking for a twelfth-hour Warwick. Even before the ink was dry on Krock's words the twelfth-hour Warwicks were appearing. Governor Baldwin of Connecticut, as yet uncommitted, arrived in Philadelphia on Sunday, June 23, and after consultation with his delegation and with Sam Pryor announced that because of popular demand and the war issue he was backing Willkie. Another important Sunday shift took place when Mayor Rolland B. Marvin of Syracuse, New York, formerly a Gannett supporter, came into the Willkie camp. Mayor Marvin, like Baldwin, was influenced by the foreign situation.

Governor Carr of Colorado joined the Willkie forces on Monday. He had been leaning toward Willkie for several weeks and was converted because of the western Willkie sentiment and war. The *New York Times* said that Governor Carr's addition came as an answer to the attempt of the Congressional group to stir up sentiment against Mr. Willkie's nomination among the delegates from the Rocky Mountain States and in refutation to the claim that Willkie had little strength west of the Mississippi River. The professionals were joining Willkie, but it was not until the second day of the convention that a board of strategy was formed and a floor manager obtained.

Stassen, the convention keynoter, provided the spark of leadership that was needed. Although John Cowles, publisher of the *Des Moines Register and Tribune* and the *Minneapolis Star-Journal,* and Raymond Clapper, a widely syndicated columnist, had been working on Stassen for several months, he had refused to commit himself until he had given up his duties as temporary chairman. Finally, the two Cowles brothers, Willkie, and Stassen got together at one o'clock in the morning of June 25. They went over Willkie's support state by state. Then Stassen, seeing the possibility of a Willkie bandwagon, said that he would support him on the condition that he could be his floor manager. He felt that he had to be sure that there were no mistakes. Stassen made his statement at 10:55 o'clock of the same morning. His offer was made without any prefatory hint and only five minutes before the meeting of his own Minnesota delegation. The move hit the convention like a bomb; at last Willkie had a Republican of national prominence behind him.

Willkie's leg men, the ones who buttonholed the delegates during the balloting, were gradually gathering. On the day of the nominating speeches this group included: Mayor Rolland Marvin; James Allen, Kansas; Walter Hallanan, West Virginia; Sinclair Weeks, Massachusetts; Lloyd Marsh, New Jersey; James Douglas, Illinois; Edgar Queeny, Missouri; and Frank Horton, Wyoming.

The amateurs added their own particular helping hand during the convention. Through the efforts of Talbott and Root the Willkie Clubs sent letters and telegrams to the delegates demanding the nomination of Willkie. This maneuver brought 500,000 messages. The convention floor was literally knee deep in orange and blue pieces of paper. Harold J. Gallegher, a distinguished member of the New York Bar, telephoned his many associates in the American Bar Association and asked them to send telegrams to add to the avalanche.

Headquarters at a convention play an important part in the candidate's organizational scheme. The general theory is that the more space the candidate can offer, the more people he will attract. Taft held the advantage in terms of rooms, with 102; Dewey and Vandenberg were a close second with seventy; Gannett, not to be outdone, had rented the entire Harvard Club; but Willkie, the man of wealth, who had only six rooms, was badly outdone. But the cramped Willkie quarters were all a part of a hasty plan by Russell Davenport to make Willkie appear as the poor man rather than the man from Wall Street. Apart from making everyone who worked at Willkie headquarters uncomfortable, the crowded quarters did give the appearance that the delegates and spectators were mobbing just to get a look at Wendell. And Wendell gave them something to look at, with his rolled-up sleeves, tieless shirt, unpressed pants and rumpled hair.

Advertising during the convention was spontaneous and sporadic. Two of the most prominent examples appeared in the Philadelphia and Eastern newspapers and were paid for and written by Chester LaRoche, president of Rubican and Young, and Ted Patrick, a copywriter. One of these advertisements directed the delegates' attention to Willkie's rise in the Gallup poll. The other was an open letter to Joseph Pew, Pennsylvania boss, and David Ingalls, Taft's campaign manager, asking them to put country above politics and nominate Willkie.

The advertisements, the smallness of the Willkie headquarters, the pro-Willkie galleries, and the letters and telegrams added to the bandwagon psychology.

Willkie's statements and actions grew more unorthodox as the delegates and other candidates became more calculating. On the first night of the convetion Roosevelt's private train pulled in Philadelphia, and the President slept on a siding. The general reaction to this event was that it was just another Roosevelt attempt to wreck the convention, but Willkie's reaction differed. When he was informed that Roosevelt was lurking nearby, he said, "Is that so? What track is he on?" "Track Three," was the reply. "Fine! That's a great track to be on."

All day Wednesday the rumor that Herbert Hoover was against Willkie was circulated. Instead of sending one of his representatives to see the ex-President, Willkie jumped in a taxi and went himself. Immediately the rumor of Hoover's opposition was quashed. Willkie did not fear Hoover or the bosses. Joseph Pew of Pennsylvania sent an emissary with a proposal for a delegate deal. Willkie coldly informed Pew's man that if the nomination came through the bosses it would not be worth having. Willkie added: "Tell him no, as we say in Indiana, I didn't drop off the berry bushes yesterday."

Except for Willkie's activities, the first three days of the convention were dull and somber. The war in Europe still maintained the most prominent position in the newspapers and over the radio. But the convention shoved the war into the background for two days. Immediately after the Resolutions Committee Report, the nomination of candidates for President was begun with Congressman Joe Martin presiding. The roll call of states was uneventful save Indiana's hesitancy. When Indiana was reached the following exchange took place:

The Secretary of the Convention: "Indiana."

Mr. Bobbitt of Indiana: "Indiana passes."

The Permanent Chairman: "Is Indiana sure that it wishes to pass?"

Mr. Bobbitt of Indiana: "Indiana passes, yes." At the conclusion of the roll call Mr. Bobbitt rose and said: "Indiana wishes to change her pass in order at the appropriate time to place in nomination Wendell Willkie." (Great applause.) On the surface this hesitation appeared to be an astute move by the Willkie backers. In reality, is was another example of the disorganized nature of the Willkie strategy. Halleck of Indiana was shaky about the nomination until Davenport assured him that he would write his nominating speech; and Halleck even then did not give his consent to deliver the address until the last minute.

The men placed in nomination were District Attorney Thomas Dewey, newspaper publisher Frank Gannett, Senator Robert Taft, Wendell Willkie, Governor Arthur Capper, Senator Styles Bridges, Oregon's Senator Charles McNary (the eventual Vice-Presidential candidate), Iowa's Senator Hanford MacNider, Pennsylvania's Governor Arthur James, and Governor Harlan Bushfield of South Dakota.

Dewey was the first to be nominated. The Dewey speeches were, for the most part, reviews of his gang-busting activities. Gannett, the second man to be put before the convention, was portrayed as an orthodox Republican. Mrs. Adele Arbo of California, who gave one of Gannett's seconding speeches, took an indirect shot at Willkie. "He

[Gannett] has everything that a Republican should have, and Republicans . . . HE IS A REPUBLICAN."

Taft, the third man to be nominated, was characterized as the man of experience, the practical and stable candidate. This was a continuation of the type of approach that had been used throughout his campaign.

In his speech for Willkie, Halleck followed the hazy strategy pattern and emphasized the fact that Willkie was the people's choice and that because of this he could win. Moreover, Halleck broke with the tradition of not mentioning the candidate's name until the conclusion of the speech. In the second paragraph he said: "If anyone were to ask me what job in this convention I would like best to have, I would choose the job I have right now. I would say, I want to place in nomination before this independent body the name of the next President of the United States, Wendell Lewis Willkie." The galleries responded to this unorthodox procedure in accord with Davenport's hope for a stampede. Repeatedly, Chairman Martin had to remind the galleries that they were guests of the convention.

After the Willkie seconding speeches were concluded, the convention recessed. On the fourth day, June 27, Verene Marshall of Iowa prefaced his MacNider nomination speech by saying, "I am certain you will be relieved to know that I have just been assured by Mr. Martin and others on this platform that this is in fact a Republican convention." (Applause and boos.) Here was another attack on Willkie. It was apparently that the professionals were not going to let the delegates forget that Willkie had been a Democrat.

Thomas McCabe of Minnesota, seconding Senator Vandenberg's nomination, made a joke of the Willkie telegrams. He said that Vandenberg had not had time to campaign. "Neither has he had time to send you wires. One of our good friends, who claimed to be a specialist in publicity, said that he didn't know whether they came from above or below, but I have a faint suspicion that they came over an electrical instrument." From the tenor of this speech and the others it is obvious that the supporters of the various candidates were preoccupied with the growing Willkie boom. The professionals were aware of Willkie's rising popularity and were doing everything they could to stop it. But they apparently forgot the old adage, "It's better to receive bad publicity than none at all."

At 4:35 p.m. on June 27 the balloting began. The convention had not received word of the Taft-Dewey understanding, which was to the effect that if Dewey failed the delegates he controlled were to go to Taft. But even as the delegates began to hear of this alignment, the question was: Did Taft and Dewey control 501 votes (the number required to nominate)?

The Taft experts had the whole matter beautifully figured. On ballot one Dewey would get about 300 votes, Taft 250, and Willkie 100. On the second ballot Dewey would slip, Taft would rise to 300, and Willkie to 150. On the subsequent ballots the Dewey support would continue to go down, Willkie would reach a maximum of 200, and Taft would win after Dewey released his controlled delegates.

But something happened to disrupt this plan on the first ballot. Dewey lost thirty-one of his own New York delegation (eight more to Willkie than he had expected); and in addition twelve of New Jersey's thirty-two supposedly secure Dewey votes went to Willkie. The New York defection of eight votes to Willkie resulted from the Dewey-Simpson feud. The twelve New Jersey votes for Willkie came by virtue of Lloyd Marsh's persuasive power. Dewey's total on the first ballot was 360, Taft's 189, sixty short of the predicted 250, and Willkie's 105. Willkie's support had come from twenty-six states — a geographic spread of backing which was a great surprise to Taft and Dewey.

Ballot two, needless to say, provided further surprises. Dewey lost five more of his New York delegation and five more of his New Jersey votes to Willkie. His total slipped twenty-two votes to 338. Taft failed by ninety-seven to meet his objective of 300. Willkie rose to 171. Things were not going as the Taft faction had planned. Taft was moving like a tortoise. Dewey's loss on this ballot was a sure sign to the experts, since no candidate in United States history had ever won the nomination of a major party after losing ground on any ballot.

At the conclusion of the second ballot, a recess, which had previously been agreed to by the candidates, was called. At 8:30 p.m. the balloting was resumed. When New York was reached, Mayor Rolland Marvin, a Willkie man, asked for a poll of the delegation after the New York chairman had reported the *second ballot* totals for each candidate. Thereupon, the Dewey support from New York was split wide open. The result of the poll doubled Willkie's total from this state, bringing it to twenty-seven, and Dewey lost four more of New York's precious votes. New Hampshire's Styles Bridges, as had been planned by the Willkie supporters and Bridges, released his delegates and four of the eight switched to Willkie. The important change on this ballot came when fifteen of Boss Pew's following ditched Governor James, the Pew candidate, and voted for Willkie. Another addition came Willkie's way when Chairman Joe Martin released his twenty-one "favorite son" delegates and twenty of them went for Willkie.

Taft gained only nine votes over his second ballot total; Dewey, still losing, went to 315; and Willkie with 259 moved ahead of Taft who had 212, and within easy striking distance of Dewey.

The fourth ballot was crucial. Dewey began to release some of his delegates. He fell to 250, thus sealing his defeat. Taft made his largest gain to that point, forty-two, pushing him to 254. But Willkie's rise continued. He was over the 300 mark by six; however, on this ballot he only gained six more votes than Taft. Even though the Taft and Willkie gains in terms of numbers were close, this vote clearly indicated that Willkie had not reached his maximum strength. In fact, he had 100 more votes than the Taft men figured he would ever get.

The nomination contest was now definitely between Taft and Willkie. On this ballot Dewey had been able to transfer about forty of his delegates to Taft. The question remaining was whether Dewey controlled the rest of his support sufficiently so that they would shift to Taft on the fifth ballot.

By the fifth ballot the tension was tremendous. The galleries were screaming the refrain, "We Want Willkie." The professionals clearly realized that they were waging a last-ditch stand. The Willkie amateurs were working at a feverish pitch — their goal was in sight. The forgotten convention, which had been shoved to the background by the European war, held the undivided attention of the nation.

It was on the fifth ballot that Dewey released the bulk of his delegates. They scattered and he was left with only fifty-four votes. His supposedly controlled New York delegation went overwhelmingly to Willkie. In New York, Dewey retained six, Taft gained five, and Willkie received thirty, which boosted his New York total to seventy-five. Kansas, ahead of New York on the roll call, went for Willkie. Alf Landon and John Hamilton had waited until this critical ballot to exert their control. Willkie now had the open support of the party's titular leaders: Alf Landon; the national chairman, John Hamilton; and the leading Republican in the House of Representatives, Joe Martin. Despite this powerful Willkie support, the gains of Taft and Willkie were equal, each added 123 votes. Although Taft had received a large share of the Dewey votes, Dewey was not able to control his backers to the extent that Taft had hoped, and approximately one-half of them went to Willkie.

The relationship between the amateurs and the professionals was at the point of breaking into open fist fights on this ballot. The resentment of the Taft backers was evidenced in the announcing of Washington's vote. "Washington casts sixteen votes for a REAL REPUBLICAN,

Senator Robert Taft." (Applause and Boos.) Chairman Martin came to Willkie's defense and said: "Characterizations of this kind are out of place here. This is a Republican convention, all the candidates are Republicans."

On the sixth ballot only two blocks of votes remained to be broken, Boss Pew's fifty Pennsylvania votes and Vandenberg's thirty-eight Michigan delegates. The Michigan block broke first and went to Wendell Willkie. This was due largely to the efforts of John Hamilton and Harold Stassen. By virtue of the Michigan shift, Willkie was assured of 460 votes. When Oregon was reached it was announced that Senator McNary had released his delegates and that they were voting for Wendell Lewis Willkie. At the conclusion of the roll call, Willkie had 499 votes, two less than were needed to nominate. Pennsylvania, which, in passing, had stimulated the galleries to shout "Deal," came in and gave its entire vote to Willkie. This was enough to give Willkie the nomination and the remaining Taft delegates rapidly changed their vote to Willkie.

Governor Bricker of Ohio, after the states had changed their vote, moved that the nomination be made unanimous. This motion was seconded by J. Russel Sprague, Senator Thomas of Idaho, Governor James of Pennsylvania and David Ingalls.

Just nine hours and seven minutes after the balloting had begun the Republicans had made their choice. It was a tremendous victory for Willkie and his amateurs. But the event was, as H. L. Mencken wrote, "shot through with evidence of a miracle. At one time I actually saw an angel in the gallery reserved for Philadelphia street railway curve greasers. To be sure, the angel had on a palm beach suit, but nevertheless it was clearly an angel." Figuratively the nomination might be called a miracle, and as such it was only one of the many from which Willkie had benefitted.

WHY THEY WANTED WILLKIE

In the late 1940's Columbia released a record called, "I Can Hear It Now," narrated by Edward R. Murrow, on which was transcribed a portion of the 1940 Republican convention. This transcript, however fragmentary, affords a glimpse of the mounting excitement, the noise and turbulence, and color which dominated the last three days of the convention. As the hulking and rumple-haired amateur, after he had received the nomination, entered the convention hall like a triumphant Caesar, there rose the refrain, its vowels prolonged to an insistent and unrelenting chant, "We want Willkie." On Murrow's record, one hears it echoed by thousands of voices; audible even at one point from the otherwise taciturn professional politician, Joseph Martin.

Why did they, the professionals, the amateurs, and the people want Willkie? As Turner Catledge observed after the convention "that he [Willkie] received the Republican nomination will long be cited as a miracle in politics, and millions of words will be used by observers in explaining it." There is little doubt that there were many intangible elements which influenced the delegates at Philadelphia, but when the whole picture is viewed one is able to discern these intangibles and their effect on the nomination. In retrospect, it almost seems that Willkie's nomination had to come.

The war in Europe was the most important single reason for the Republican choice. However, the war had little influence on American public opinion until the first of May, 1940. It enhanced Willkie's availability.

In addition to the war many factors were at work prior to May, 1940, which made him a serious contender. Willkie's rise to prominence is best explained by the anomalous nature of our party system. Basically political parties in the United States are non-ideological. Men and groups move in and out of our major parties with each shift of the political winds. In reality, Willkie came into the Republican party and the titular leadership thereof because he and powerful segments of the New Deal coalition were changing their political allegiance.

The assumption of the presidency of Commonwealth and Southern after the economic collapse of 1933 made it possible for Willkie to become a depression success. Because of this he was not associated with any of the bitter past of big business. He provided the most spectacular and unorthodox business leadership of the day. In his stand on social and economic reform, he vied with some of the most ardent New Dealers. Yet, he fought the New Deal whenever the theory of government threatened his preserve. Moreover, he was one of the few business men to gain any Washington victories. As a utilities executive and a former New Freedom Democrat he believed that government, business, or any other group should not be let to exercise unchecked political power.

A philosophy such as this, a magnetic personality and a position of leadership made it inevitable that his political potency would be recognized. As he spoke and wrote, many people began to realize that Willkie was a man with whom they could agree. The support that he received during the 1930's was a result of two things — first, the troubled times and Willkie's reaction to them, and second, a spontaneous reaction to Willkie himself. He was talking in terms of ideas. His reaction to the New Deal was one which many were experiencing. "But the thing I am most interested in is ideas. I am frankly trying to win popular support for principles in which I believe. You know, twenty or thirty years ago I was in the fight against 'big business' and the monopolies. I was in it with all my heart . . . To me today we have the same kind of fight for the preservation of the people's liberties except that 'big business' has now been licked and today it is 'big government' . . ." He literally said what many of the people were thinking.

The spontaneous reaction to Willkie demonstrated the American capacity to discover new men. On the other hand, Willkie had the ability to stimulate and recognize the ill-defined forces of American life which affected himself and others. This two-way process is a study of the function of leadership in a democratic society.

Aside from having a domestic and social philosophy with which the people could agree, Willkie was the only Republican aspirant who consistently stated that our fate was interwoven with that of the European democracies. It would be difficult to defend the proposition that the delegates in Philadelphia were continuously aware of Europe. Most of them were concerned with the drama in which they were participating.

In the small hours of the morning one delegate was heard to say to another, "What's going on in the outside world? I haven't read a newspaper headline all week." In a sense, however, Philadelphia and the Republican convention were under remote control of Europe. The delegates were subconsciously aware of the real dangers of war. Behind the Willkie landslide there was an intangible desire for assurance of security, for preparedness to meet any possible contingencies that the war in Europe might bring. The *New York Times* claimed that "Wendell Willkie was nominated on a wave of revulsion against the kind of political sclerosis revealed in France as the hurricane broke." The old world was rapidly falling. The United States was without a wall of defense and exposed to dangers as severe as it had ever faced. Because of this the Republicans could not be unrealistic and nominate an isolationist.

Willkie as a leader of business and at the same time committed to all-out aid for the Allies presented a combination much in demand. In fact, he was the only Republican who represented the changing American sentiment towards business and the war. Of course, the Republicans, in theory, could have nominated another man who was wholeheartedly pro-Ally and who accepted the principle of social and economic reform. The four men within the party who represented the position were not available: Landon, in 1936, had suffered the worst defeat in the Republican party's history; Colonel Knox joined Roosevelt's cabinet, thereby aligning himself with the party's archrival; Stimson, like Knox, put his party to one side in accepting the Secretaryship of War in Roosevelt's cabinet; Justice Roberts had let friends know that he would not permit himself to be drafted.

These four men were the only big names in the party who were in accord with Roosevelt's foreign policy. To be sure, the Republicans could have selected some lesser pro-Ally man who was a regular party member. But this is idle conjecture in view of the fact that Willkie was the only interventionist who was a popular national figure. Not since Teddy Roosevelt had the party had a real give-'em-hell campaigner; in other words, a man who was able to attract the attention of the people and hold it. The Republican party would have committed political suicide had it thrown over this man for some lesser-known internationally minded candidate.

The stand that Willkie took on foreign affairs attracted the support of the international wing of the party. This is the wing composed of the worldwide bankers, traders and manufacturers. The locus of power in this element is on the eastern seaboard. In 1940, when the European democracies began to fall, these businessmen realized that aiding the Allies was in their own best interest. They felt the effects of the European war more than any other element in the country since they did business on a world basis and had operations in close proximity to the battlefields. It was only natural that they should look for a candidate with whom they could agree on foreign policy. Willkie as a utilities executive and an internationalist was the man to whom they could most easily give their support.

Willkie's personal qualities were not recognized immediately by the public. He was a "different" personality, but there were other unusual personalities in the party and in the country. The particular and unusual facets of Willkie's character were brought to the attention of the public by skilled and subtle means. His unique physical appearance was exaggerated. His battle against the malefactors of "big government" and "big business" was rapidly built into something of a myth. This character exploitation was carried out by the organs of mass opinion. The amateurs saw that no stone was unturned in portraying Willkie as a new kind of political leader. Willkie's own catch-as-catch-can technique made him a natural master of timing releases, issuing denials, adding punch lines to speeches, making impromptu addresses that appeared to be letter perfect, and treating all men with the personal approach that suggested to each that they were the only beneficiaries of his gratitude.

Another factor in Willkie's selection was that the other candidates had practically eliminated themselves by convention time. Dewey lacked experience and at thirty-eight was thought to be too young for the job. His inexperience and youth were continuously brought up after Hitler's April invasion of the Low Countries. Moreover, there was a bit of bad psychology tied up with the above point — the prediction that he would fade because of his youth and inexperience. Dewey's appeal was to the same grass-roots people as Willkie. In this latter regard some observers say that Willkie out-Deweyed Dewey by stealing his audience. And as Dewey declined in the public opinion polls, the politicans began to whisper that he could not win the nomination or the election. With each speech Dewey made, he made himself less available. In other words, he had only mometarily captured the popular imagination. His "Dick Tracy" speeches became shallow in the face of the European crisis.

Taft had a great deal less popular appeal than Dewey. He was solid and respectable, but he was dull. There was a feeling that he would make an even less effective candidate than Landon. Further, he was, despite his early rise to Congressional leadership, inexperienced and new to national politics. And Senator Vandenberg's refusal to campaign and his overwhelming defeats in the primaries greatly deflated any chance that he might have had for the nomination.

The most serious drawback of all three defeated candidates — Taft, Dewey, and Vandenberg — was the fact that they were isolationists. Taft did acknowledge the need for preparedness, but he was opposed to aid for the Allies. Dewey had been an isolationist until the latter part of May. When he finally emerged from his shell and advocated aid to the European democracies it was too late. Willkie's candidacy, as indicated by public opinion polls, was growing into a bandwagon because of his support of the Allies. Moreover, the question was raised as to Dewey's sincerity. He had been caught in a trap. If he had maintained his neutral attitude he would have been considered no worse than the traditional Republican isolationist, whereas his change had the earmarks of a purely political move. Senator Vandenberg, in a sense, was the most outspoken isolationist of all. His policy of insulation was looked upon by many as an extreme form of isolationism.

Franklin Roosevelt had an effect on the Republican choice. The Stimson and Knox appointments focused attention on the foreign situation. This move indicated the gravity of the situation. But more important than this was the fact that the Republicans felt that Roosevelt would be the Democratic nominee. Two days before the Republicans met in Philadelphia the *New York Times* reported that Roosevelt had seven hundred pledged delegates, and if he was not going to accept the nomination he would have to repudiate this support.

Had the threat of Roosevelt not been hanging over the Republican delegates there is a possibility that someone else might have been nominated. It is probable that the G.O.P. bosses might have been bolder and the demand for a candidate with punch and color less important. However, the delegates realized that the Republican party would have to have someone with dynamic appeal to offset Roosevelt's campaign techniques.

Important in Willkie's victory was the fact that the delegates were not effectively controlled. The bosses made the mistake of assuming that the majority of the delegates was in their political pockets. In their confidence they forgot that the delegates could reason and act upon their own convictions. Of course, delegates do not always think for themselves, but the fallacy consists in supposing that they never do. As the delegates began to convene there was a growing realization of the uselessness of attempting to win an election with an opposition organization. This had been, many felt, a factor in the 1936 defeat. The party needed an opposition candidate who could assume leadership. Willkie more and more appeared to be the best possible opposition candidate.

In attempting to explain the 1940 miracle the work of the political amateurs must be included. Their schemes of writing chain letters, sending telegrams to the delegates, packing the galleries, and selecting a small Philadelphia headquarters added to the psychology that Willkie was the people's choice. Of course, there was the impact of Willkie's personality on the delegates. The number of those who were affected by his magnetism will never be known, but to say that none voted for him for this reason is to underestimate the potential of the Willkie personality. The work of the professionals, regardless of their motivation, was a necessary part of the convention manipulation.

The spectacular rise of Willkie to a position of national prominence was well timed. He was like a great salesman who believed in himself and transferred his assurance to others. He and his enthusiastic amateurs threw deep shadows over the deficiencies in his experience and potentialities. In the four years that followed the nomination, the shadows disappeared and his weaknesses stood starkly revealed. The delegates could not have foreseen that Willkie lacked cooperativeness and the ability to work with a political team. Because of his free-lance thinking he was a poor political security. The Republicans accepted Willkie because they did not know him and as they got to know him they dropped him. Willkie's was a virtuoso role. He was swept to the top mainly because of the exigencies of the European war. As far as the Republican party was concerned Willkie's leadership was short lived.

His political ineptness notwithstanding, Willkie could know that his party despite rejecting his leadership, has embraced most of the objectives for which he fought so gallantly and, it seemed, so hopelessly. He could also know that he gave the annals of politics one of its brightest and most unbelievable pages. In more ways than one, Willkie's nomination signified a shift within the Republican party. In effect, 1940 was the beginning of the Old Guard's last stand. Philadelphia was the first of a long and continuing series of battles between the economic liberal internationalist easterner and the economic conservative isolationist midwesterner.

Willkie's nomination was one of the historical turning points in the life of the Republican party. Basically there are two ways in which a party can meet the challenge of new ideas and the realignment of forces. The first is to continue in the old pattern, nominating a man who is a national figure and obscure the issues through a campaign of ballyhoo. In selecting William Henry Harrison, the Whigs of 1840 adopted this technique. They did not broaden the base of their appeal to meet the demands of the agrarian West and South, but nominated a war hero who was in the Federalist-National Republican tradition. By doing this the Whig party continued as a spokesman for the commercial, financial, and big planter groups.

The second way in which a party adapts to new forces and conditions is by broadening its base of appeal. This method was used very successfully by Theodore Roosevelt. True, the Republicans were forced to nominate him for the Vice-Presidency in order to get him out of the political way; however, in 1901, upon McKinley's death, he ascended to the Presidency and proceeded to catch the Republican party up with the times. Roosevelt's vigorous, sometimes ineffectual conservation and anti-trust policies appealed to the pressures which were manifest in that day.

In 1940 the party reached another historical turning point. The social and economic forces unleashed by the depression and war had to be dealt with if the Republicans were to accomplish a group coalition which would return them to power. As I pointed out in the first chapter, the party was split over methods to be used in effecting a basis of support which would enable them to recapture national leadership. After seven years of attempting to win popular support with traditional policies, the Republicans at Philadelphia nominated Willkie, who represented the changing American attitude on domestic and foreign affairs. Willkie's nomination was a compromise between factions within the party, but more important it was a realization, by a majority of Republicans, that the party had to broaden its appeal and wean away a portion of the Democratic coalition in order to return to power.

At best, Willkie's nomination was an uneasy and a temporary settlement of the problem. Since 1940 there has been a recurrence of the battle between the traditional "laissez faire" isolationists and those who favor government intervention and internationalism. To be sure, the conservative isolationists are neither as conservative nor as isolationist as they were in 1940. The more enlightened members of this group provide a healthy opposition to the proponents of economic liberalism and internationalism. Contrariwise, the latter group, by forcing the party to adopt a more liberal stand on domestic and foreign affairs, serves as a means whereby the party can offer programs which enable it to appeal to a wider group. Since 1940, despite the basic differences of opinion between the factions, they have operated in the

Republican party and the democratic frame of reference. The battles are examples of how a pluralistic democracy can solve its problem without compelling opposition to adopt a particular point of view.

It is evident that the Willkie nomination in 1940, the Dewey nominations in 1944 and 1948, the Eisenhower nominations in 1952 and 1956, and the Nixon nomination in 1960 have represented a slow but unbroken transfer of control from the Old Guard Republicans to the modern Republicans. At each convention, a liberal and an internationalist candidate were victorious. Up to the present time the conservative Republicans have not been able to win the nomination, but in the 1944 and 1952 conventions the Taft margin of defeat was slim. They still hold a series of powerful party and elective offices. The question, then, that remains to be answered is: Does this shift represent a permanent change or will it be reversed at the 1964 convention?

Thomas in the Detroit News

"After All She Has Said About Glamour Boys"

THE DECADES OF ACCOMMODATION: 1940–60

In the haste and confusion of Philadelphia many Republican delegates had been carried forward on the crest of a tidal wave of popular support for Willkie. During the campaign of 1940 and afterward, until Willkie's death in 1944, the Republican party was led by a man who was unashamed of his espousal of many New Deal goals and who was committed to what for most Republicans was a complete anathema — "One World" — in international affairs. After 1940 the Republicans would not make the mistake of nominating a political free-lancer like Willkie; even so they could not throw off Willkie's imprint. The party was never to be the same.

Despite the vigorous campaign Willkie waged in 1940 he could not overcome the strong attachment of farmers and laborers to Roosevelt. Moreover the same consideration — the gravity of the world situation — which had caused many to advocate his nomination was a major factor in influencing the voters to support Roosevelt as a proven leader. In addition to these factors, Willkie's campaign was confused and disorganized. These same two elements had been present in his contest for the nomination, and they had seemed to help rather than hinder him. However, in a nationwide campaign in which voters had to be given strong reasons for breaking their traditional loyalties, confusion and disorganization made it appear that Willkie was not capable of national leadership. Even with these liabilities Willkie polled more votes than any previous Republican presidential candidate. He had cut the President's margin in half and had garnered more votes than Dewey would in 1944 or 1948.

One week after the election, Willkie issued a patriotic call to all Republicans, designating their proper role as that of the "loyal opposition." A number of Republican official organizations considered resolutions condemning Willkie. The publicity director of the Republican

National Committee claimed that "loyal" and "opposition" were contrary concepts, and that "they do not make sense." In the weeks that followed Willkie made it clear that his greatest personal effort was to be in the direction of loyalty and not opposition. For instance, he backed lend-lease aid for England. This stand brought forth a storm of protest from Republican leaders. Alf Landon in a bit of hindsight, contended that Willkie, like Roosevelt, would go to war to help England, and that had he revealed this prior to the convention "he would not have been nominated."

The Republicans in the House of Representatives appeared to reaffirm Landon's contention when one-sixth of them voted against the lend-lease bill. The House Republicans were joined by two-thirds of their colleagues in the Senate in opposing the bill. As late as November 13, 1941, a large majority of the congressional Republicans voted against repeal of the Neutrality Act. In view of the prevailing temper of the times, the isolationist recalcitrance of Republican legislators is difficult to comprehend. According to Gallup polls even the most isolationist areas in the U.S. appear to have had serious doubts about maintaining non-involvement in the strife-torn world of late 1940. In March, 1941, the conservative *Magazine of Wallstreet* charged that Republicans had failed "to grasp the significance of world events or to keep in tune with public sentiment."

In part, the Old Guard stand of congressional Republicans can be explained because of their commitment to criticism of Roosevelt. Undoubtedly, they were counting on an anti-war sentiment which would return them to power. There was also the desire to clip Willkie's political wings. In opposing Roosevelt whom Willkie was supporting, Republican leaders were making it clear that they were not going to have a repeat performance of 1940. But even the isolationists in the party were to be diverted from traditional patterns of thought. Indeed, it is an interesting commentary on U.S. politics that it took a direct attack on the country to bring this about-face. Senator Vandenberg spoke for many of them when he said: "In my own mind, my convictions regarding international cooperation and collective security for peace took form on the afternoon of the Pearl Harbor attack. That day ended isolationism for any realist." When the Republican National Committee met in the spring of 1942, it had no alternative but to heed Willkie's call for postwar international cooperation.

After biding his time on the issue, Thomas E. Dewey, by now Governor of New York, took this opportunity to announce that he had been for international cooperation all along. By this time public opinion polls revealed that Dewey was the choice of 53 per cent of the Republican voters for the nomination in 1944. Shortly after the spring meeting of the Republican National Committee, Dewey and Vandenberg endorsed a "bi-partisan foreign policy"; something which Willkie had in effect called for two years previously.

Despite the change of heart of many Republicans on the international and domestic policies of Roosevelt, Harrison Spangler was elected National Chairman in 1942. Spangler announced that his job was to defeat the New Deal, and that the votes to do this could not be found in Mongolia or Russia. On the domestic scene, Spangler called for a return to constitutional government and "away from totalitarianism and state socialism." Disdaining the "me-too-ism" of Vandenberg, Dewey and Willkie, Spangler called for an end to bureaucratic hampering of business and a return to free enterprise. These notions were set forth in an article by Spangler in the *American Magazine* for February, 1943 which carried the interesting and, to some, amazing title, "The G.O.P.'s New Stand."

Regardless of his own views, Spangler realized that if the party was to countenance hopes of presidential victory in 1944, all factions within the party would have to close ranks. With this view in mind, Spangler called for an advisory council to meet at Mackinac Island to discuss postwar problems. The party's three living presidential nominees, Hoover, Landon, and Willkie, were not issued invitations in the hope that the conference could concentrate on policies that could return them to power rather than on personalities. At the conference, Republican governors took the initiative from the congressional leaders and solidly supported a Willkie-oriented program which pledged the party to support U.S. cooperation in a postwar international organization.

Not to be stymied completely, some Old Guarders formed a Republican Nationalist Revival Committee to counteract the internationalism of the progressives. The "Nationalist" label was adopted because it carried a more favorable public reaction than "isolation." In addition to neo-isolationism, the committee advanced the causes of states' rights and decentralization of government power.

In the midst of these developments Dewey appeared to vacillate. He alternately opposed and supported portions of the Mackinac declaration. In reality, he was pursuing a course similar to the one he had followed in the months before the 1940 convention. This time he was more skilled and more effective. The tables were now turned in Dewey's favor. In 1940 Dewey's public pronouncements had seriously damaged his availability. During the interlude between 1940 and 1944 it was

Willkie who through his loyal opposition speeches and actions had precluded the 1944 convention fom nominating him.

The skill with which Dewey handled his pre-convention activities is attested by the fact that he was nominated on the first ballot. Dewey's political coyness had paid off, but it was still to present problems for him. To have any chance against Roosevelt, Dewey would have to adopt a firm liberal-internationalist stand akin to Willkie's position. For Dewey, as Willkie had been, was confronted with the necessity of weaning away members from the Roosevelt coalition. It also appeared crucial that the 1944 platform meet with Willkie's approval.

As the convention developed, however, it became apparent that while the pro-Willkie governors could control the nomination, the congressional wing of the party would formulate the platform. Taft supporters who controlled much of the convention machinery had formulated the party's program. One observer contends that they did not consult with the Dewey men on the platform. If this was the case, Dewey did not protest and tacitly accepted an international plank unacceptable to Willkie. The rejected leader condemned the plank as doing nothing more than paying lip service to internationalism.

As he had done throughout his career, Willkie used the periodicals as the outlet for his condemnation of what he considered to be equivocation on basic issues. He did concede that his party had the better domestic policy, but he was frank in his preference for the Democratic foreign policy. In part, Willkie's approval of the domestic program of his party was based on the fact that the Republicans had appropriated much of the New Deal. Thirty planks of the 1944 platform had been taken directly from the achievements of the Roosevelt administration. It is a tribute to Willkie's powers of persuasion that as his series of articles was published, Dewey's speeches grew closer to the program Willkie was suggesting.

The process of accommodation through Willkie was halted abruptly when he died on October 7, 1944. Meanwhile, Dewey raced down the homestretch. Unable to engage Roosevelt on the issues, because Roosevelt would not be so engaged, Dewey began to hint that the Roosevelt administration was tainted by Communism. In a carefully worded speech Dewey linked Communists with the incumbent administration. Three million copies of this speech were alleged to have been distributed during the campaign.

It was all to no avail. If Willkie had been too frank, Dewey had been too ambivalent on the issues. It was not until after Pearl Harbor that he had become a thoroughgoing internationalist. And even this conversion was to be seriously questioned until the 1944 campaign. In 1944, he attempted to efface the taint of isolationist association by declaring strongly for international cooperation after the war. But the Republican platform was not as clear on the issue as the party's candidate, and Willkie had pointed this out. Dewey eventually found the Republican congressional record, even after Pearl Harbor, to be an insurmountable burden. To the voter, there was still little to indicate that the Republicans could lead in war or the peace that was growing more of a certainty with each Allied success. The plight of the Republicans was clearly indicated when Senator Ball of Minnesota announced his support of Roosevelt during the last week of the campaign. Ball's decision was based on the international situation and the relative ability of Roosevelt and Dewey to handle it.

When the votes were counted, Dewey had decreased Roosevelt's popular margin, but had carried only two more states than had Willkie. It appeared to many Republicans that the party could never be successful against Roosevelt in a national election contest. He had beaten them four times, and now they could only hope that they would not have to face him again. As has happened frequently in American politics, death of the President created new visions of success in the minds of the minority party members. Harold Gosnell has labelled Roosevelt "the great campaigner," and the politically battle-weary Republicans of 1945 could give testimony to this label. If Roosevelt had been a great campaigner, there were many Republicans who after the 1948 elections would have called his successor, Harry Truman, the "greatest campaigner."

The reasons for this are not hard to discover. In the off-year election of 1946 the Republicans gained control of both houses of Congress for the first time in 16 years. The Republicans made great use of the slogan, "Had enough? Vote Republican!" Undoubtedly, reaction to the war and the party that had been in power throughout it had carried the Republicans to victory in 1946. Odds were that this trend would continue and sweep *any* Republican to the presidency in 1948. This belief was given credence when the Progressives and the Dixiecrats bolted the Democratic party.

Somewhat complacent, the Republicans were not exultant about Dewey's candidacy. However, his opponents could not agree on an alternative. Taft supporters would take Dewey before Stassen, and Stassen delegates preferred Dewey to Taft. Dewey having preserved his role as titular head of the party between 1944 and 1948 was the easiest choice. In order to accentuate the changed nature of the party, Governor Earl Warren, an avowed liberal, was chosen as Dewey's running mate.

In addition to a popular and progressive running mate, Dewey had a platform aimed at wooing the laborers from the Roosevelt coalition. It called for acceptance of the labor statutes of the Roosevelt era, expansion of social security and a guarantee of full employment. Senator Vandenberg had taken the lead in advocating a foreign policy program which rejected isolationism as an archaic legacy of the past. He was joined by other Senate Republicans in advocating economic and military assistance for Europe. Senator Vandenberg expressed the hope that the 1948 platform would forever remove the isolationist stigma from the Republican party. In essence, the Republican convention pledged the party's support for foreign aid, the United Nations and reciprocal tariffs.

Dewey and the party leaders were confident that their forward-looking ticket and platform would assure them of victory. But they had not counted on the political skill of their adversary. In a stroke of political genius Truman called the Eightieth Congress into special session and challenged the Republican majority to make good on its platform promises. The Republicans reacted just as Truman thought they would and rejected his call to action. In the September, 1948 issue of *Harper's,* Elmer Davis took note of Dewey's strange "bedfellows." He predicted that the Eightieth Congress would be the "glass jaw of the Republican party," and that Democrats would poke away at it all during the campaign.

As Truman blasted away at the "do nothing Eightieth Congress" in his "give-'em-hell' style the American voters came to have second thoughts about rejecting Roosevelt's hand-picked successor. Truman fed these incipient doubts by charging that the Republican Congress had taken 750,000 people off the social security rolls. The record of the Republican Congressmen was once again to cause Dewey great difficulty. Dewey might have assuaged these doubts by waging a vigorous campaign, but as one observer said, he acted as if he were the President instead of running for the job. He was confident that the opinion polls were correct and preferred platitudes and smirks to specific commitments.

On election day, a combination of Old Guard obstreperousness and Dewey's own timidity were obstacles the Republicans could not overcome. Garnering a minority of popular votes, Truman nonetheless secured a clear electoral majority. Except for the defection of the Dixiecrats and the Progressives, the New Deal coalition had remained tenuously intact. A light turnout probably indicated disillusionment among the voters and was a danger signal for the Democrats in 1952. At any rate, Thomas Dewey's ten-year quest for the presidency had come to an end. He would continue campaigning for Republican national candidates. And there are many within the party who say that his campaign efforts on behalf of the Republican ticket in either 1952 or 1960 would have won the 1948 election had he possessed the foresight to use them.

The reaction to Dewey's defeat in the conservative camp of the party was violent. Dewey had lost a "cinch" election. Die-hards claimed that "me-tooism" had alienated the staunch Republican voters, causing them to stay at home rather than have to vote for a Republican reincarnation of Roosevelt. In retrospect it can be said that if anything it was the Democrats torn by the three-way split in their own party who had stayed at home. For instance, as Samuel Lubell points out, "for Dewey to squeeze by in New York state by a mere 55,000 votes, Truman had to lose 520,000 Roosevelt votes. In New York City every third or fourth Roosevelt voter appears to either have stayed at home or voted for Wallace."

Mistaken or not, Republican reaction was in full sway by December, 1949. A year after the election a special G.O.P. strategy committee voted unanimously to wipe out all vestiges of "me-tooism." Members of the committee included Leonard Hall and Arthur Summerfield, respectively Party Chairman and Postmaster General during the Eisenhower presidency. Both later converted to the "new Republicanism" of President Eisenhower. The strategy committee also declared that they were irreconcilably opposed to the welfare state. Even Senator Taft was taken to task for supporting federal aid to education and public housing. Asked about Taft's possible reaction to such criticism, a committee member said that "it was just too damn bad for Taft."

This condemnation was certainly not indicative of a stampede to liberalism by the senator from Ohio. In fact, during the 1950–51 confusion, the Taft wing began making isolationist sounds once more. Taft spoke of our "traditional policy of neutrality and non-interference" and inveighed against foreign policy expenses.

Despite these developments, all was not dark on the horizon of "modern Republicanism." Strident new progressive spokesmen were emerging. Among these was Henry Cabot Lodge, Jr., who elucidated principles which must have caused his Old Guard father to revolve in his tomb. In the March, 1950, issue of the *Atlantic Monthly,* Lodge undertook to offer specific proposals to "modernize" the G.O.P. He rejected Old Guard tenets as being "anchored to a dead past." Lodge foresaw defeat as the inevitable price of adherence to the outdated "Mossback" philosophy. In a definite break with Republican tradition, he stressed the need for a strong President such as Roosevelt. By way of a definite program, Lodge proposed modification of the Taft-Hartley Act, inceased old-age and health benefits, and *a guaranteed annual wage to stabilize employment*. Thus, within Republican ranks, reaction raged on one hand, and liberalism surged forward on the other. The countervailing tendencies were sure to collide in the 1952 convention.

The portended clash occurred at the presidential nominating convention in Chicago. Bitter though the battle was, its result was practically a foregone conclusion. Though the conservatives controlled much of the party machinery and had the candidate of principle, the progressives had the delegate votes and the candidate who could win. The contest was almost academic. Supporters of Senator Taft named all important convention posts from keynoter Douglas MacArthur down to the assistant doorkeepers. But twenty-three of twenty-five Republican state governors were supporting General Dwight Eisenhower, whom public opinion polls had shown to be the leading presidential candidate, regardless of party.

Since the Republicans had enjoyed no federal patronage in twenty years, the support of the governors was crucial. The mere threat of an influential governor such as Dewey to hold his patronage in abeyance was sufficient to quiet rebellious delegates within his state's contingent. Using such threats as a fulcrum, the governors propelled "Ike" into a first ballot nomination. The Vice-Pesidential nominee was young Senator Richard M. Nixon of California. Because of his role in apprehending Alger Hiss, it was assumed that Nixon had captured the popular imagination and as was the case with Warren represented the growing political importance of the western half of the U.S.

Eisenhower's nomination was a victory for the progressive wing of the party, but no one really knew whether he was liberal or conservative. Frustrated Taft supporters jibed, "We like Ike, but what's Ike like?" This lack of political commitment was a great asset to Eisenhower during the convention and especially during the campaign. Taft's greatest liability was that everyone knew what he was like. He had taken a forthright conservative stand on so many issues, that his candidacy would probably have solidified the New Deal coalition on every front. In contrast, Eisenhower's appeal was basically personal and apolitical. It was Governor Fine of Pennsylvania who best summed up the reason Eisenhower was nominated. The governor said that Eisenhower was the candidate who offered "the least risk of failure." Shortly after the campaign began in earnest, Eisenhower and Taft met to insure party harmony. They agreed that the major campaign issue was "liberty against creeping socialism."

As the campaign proceeded, the Republican issues conformed to Dewey's formula K^1C^2; Korea, corruption, and Communism. All three issues were extraneous to economics, which suited the G.O.P. well. Since 1932 the Republicans had been haunted in every election year by the spectre of the Great Depression; this year it was going to be different. And it was. By 1952, many victims of the depression had risen to middle class economic status. Continued prosperity had dimmed their memories of privation and had stimulated within them a powerful urge for tranquility. They were no longer so much interested in increasing their economic gains as in securing what they had already won. More and more the new middle class was concerned about the effects of inflation upon their savings. On the whole, the middle class longed for the contentment and stability of a modern "Normalcy."

Eisenhower seemed sympathetic toward these yearnings. He promised to maintain New Deal gains but also to reduce taxes and to curb inflation. After offering this solace to middle class economic frustrations, Eisenhower was free to harp on the "special issues" of 1952: Korea, corruption, and Communism.

The anti-Communist appeal sought to accentuate the disillusionment of many Democrats with the Roosevelt-Truman foreign policy. In so doing, the Republicans suggested that most of the foreign policy blunders attendant to World War II had been the result of Communist intrigue and subversion. Such a viewpoint would naturally have appeal among former anti-Roosevelt isolationists. But Eisenhower's appeal was not limited. Having served as Supreme Allied Commander during World War II, he could also command the allegiance of those who had *supported* Roosevelt's foreign policy.

Thus the apparent paradox in the 1952 voting pattern, which found Eisenhower gaining in both isolationist and interventionist strongholds. The greatest Republican gains were registered in former isolationist areas, populated chiefly by Germans and Italians who had opposed United States intervention in World War II. But Eisenhower also realized significant gains among the former interventionists, such as the Poles and the Czechs, who were angered by Yalta and Potsdam.

In the main, however, Eisenhower was far above a return to isolationism and the guise of a "Fortress America." "Massive retaliation" provided for an emphasis on long-range nuclear power as a response to aggression. This was far superior in the minds of many to Truman's theory of "limited war." An aloof, yet seemingly effective defense, "massive retaliation" was designed to bridge the foreign policy gap between the internationalist and the isolationist wings of the G.O.P.

There was another "disillusioned" group to which Eisenhower appealed in 1952. Lured by traditional Republican support of states' rights, many disgruntled southern racists supported "Ike." In 157 Black Belt counties (where Negroes weren't allowed to vote), Eisenhower polled eight times more votes than had Dewey.

In summary, Eisenhower's victory was the product of a great ferment in many different areas of public sentiment. Torn by a maelstrom of conflicting domestic and international crosscurrents, the American people found solace in the engaging grin of a great popular hero. Eisenhower scored a smashing personal victory. Polling a majority of six million, Eisenhower won an electoral vote margin of 457–74. Significantly, the Republican party lagged far behind its champion. Though the G.O.P. enjoyed a small margin in the House of Representatives, the Senate Republicans would require the support of the "maverick" Oregonian Wayne Morse to maintain a majority. But this situation was secondary to the great fact of the 1952 election. After twenty years of absence, the Republicans were back in the White House.

As the gleeful Republicans trooped into Washington, Eisenhower assembled his cabinet. In the main, where Roosevelt had called upon "brain trusters" and Truman upon professional politicians, Eisenhower selected businessmen for his cabinet. One of these businessman administrators managed to get himself into hot water immediately. Secretary of the Treasury Humphreys set out at once to fulfill the Republican campaign pledge to curb inflation. To do so, Humphreys relied on time-honored orthodox means. Early in 1953, he lifted interest rates and tightened credit control. The tight money policy caused an immediate slump in the bond market and the Administration was forced to loosen its controls.

Undaunted by this failure, the Administration promised to decentralize economic controls. In spite of their allegedly great concern over the amount of the national debt, Republican businessmen called for a tax reduction. The Administration obligingly allowed excess profits taxes to expire and effected a reduction in personal income and business taxes by the 1954 schedule.

From this rather conservative beginning, the Eisenhower Administration moved to a more liberal position early in 1954. In his State of the Union message the President called for expanded foreign aid and trade, a four-year public housing program, and an expansion of social security. The Republicans in Congress gave first priority to the Bricker amendment and the Army-McCarthy hearings. The Bricker amendment would have severely limited the presidential power to engage in executive agreements. It was sponsored by Republican Congressmen and reflected their latent opposition to Eisenhower's progressive appearances.

Of far more serious import was the McCarthy hassle. Seizing upon the "Communists in government" issue that had been a Republican secondary theme since 1940, McCarthy was terrorizing Washington with his sensational investigations. Eisenhower's position on the matter was ticklish. McCarthy appealed to the same "disillusionist" elements that had supported "Ike" overwhelmingly in 1952. Therefore, Eisenhower could not afford to rebuke McCarthy openly, and had to ride out the Wisconsin "witch hunter's" storm in silence.

Not dismayed by Congressional setbacks, hopeful Republicans extolled the merts of "dynamic conservatism." Vice-President Nixon said that the Eisenhower Administration "will build more roads, . . . schools . . . and houses, provide better medical care, and develop more power and water resources than our predecessors ever dreamed of." Nixon stated that "we oppose the programs of our predecessors not because they were too high but because they were too low." On most fronts the Eisenhower Republicans proclaimed their progressivism.

Many of these "modern Republicans" were actually sincere progressives. In some instances there was cause for doubt. Leonard Hall, ultra-conservative strategist of 1949, was now party chairman. He was being described as a thoroughly convinced Eisenhowerite. Perhaps the motives behind Mr. Hall's conversion may best be assessed by his own words. "In the past we have been accused of opposing social progress. This charge can never be made again. Under the leadership of President Eisenhower we are becoming the party of social progress."

Congressional Republicans were not so *blasé* in their acceptance of Eisenhower's programs. After the Republicans lost control of Congress in the 1954 elections, an intraparty battle ensued. It centered around the motion to censure McCarthy. As the debate proceeded, the Republicans' deep cleavage over foreign affairs became apparent. Most of the Old Guard stuck by McCarthy, and Republican Floor Leader William Knowland sharply criticized the Eisenhower-Dulles foreign policy.

All such differences were minimized as the Republicans went to convention in 1956. Eisenhower's renomination was a foregone conclusion. Stassen introduced some excitement by initiating a "dump Nixon" move which never materialized. There were no startling innovations proposed by the 1956 platform. One wag quipped, "If a platform could have been written with the word "Ike" it would have been."

On election day Eisenhower swept to a victory of Rooseveltian proportions as he polled 57 per cent of the popular vote. For the first time in a century, a President elected with a popular majority failed to carry along a Congress of his own party. Eisenhower accepted the thesis that it was a personal triumph, and privately commented that the public was not yet convinced of the G.O.P.'s conversion to "modern Republicanism."

This belief gained further credence as the first session of the Eighty-Fifth Congress opened. The fortunes of Eisenhower Republicans were on the wane and the Old Guard was resurging. A conservative coalition between the Old Guard and the southern conservatives was the deciding factor on many issues. Progressive Republicans were relegated to unimportant positions. Since Eisenhower dealt with Congress through regular, therefore conservative, channels, he lost rapport with his own supporters.

Operating under a severe handicap because of the twenty-second amendment, Eisenhower disdained using his immense personal popularity to obtain passage of his legislative programs. He was undoubtedly prone to the Republican fondness for a weak president. Max Ascoli sardonically commented that the "G.O.P. has been running the country by a combination of collective leadership and Eisenhower's personality." Unfortunately, neither the collective leadership nor Eisenhower's personality were coping effectively with the great issues of the day.

The administration vacillated on modern Republicanism and made a number of serious mistakes. Instead of facilitating a flexible adjustment to the fluctuations of the business cycle, Eisenhower desired that the budget be balanced annually, even in a year of recession. To balance the budget in 1958, Eisenhower reduced farm price supports and outlays for public works. Unfortunately, this cutback in government spending coincided with an economic recession. The consequences were catastrophic for Republican Congressmen in 1958. In the mid-term elections, the Democrats swept to a landslide victory. Many Democrats were heartened by what they read as a protest against those in power.

Hard on the heels of the Congressional defeat came new foreign policy reverses. Capitalizing upon the tremendous psychological advantages accrued to their scientific successes, the Russians audaciously seized the initiative on all international fronts. Momentarily successful at Geneva in 1955, the famed Eisenhower smile was no longer a potent force. As the presidential year of 1960 rolled around, certain sober reflections on the Eisenhower presidency could not be avoided. Disregarding the issues peculiar to the 1952 campaign, three issues had impelled the moderates to support Eisenhower: foreign policy, racial tolerance, and economic stability. Eienhower had not enjoyed spectacular success on any of these counts.

Many had voted for Eisenhower in 1952 in protest against the southern Democrats' minority zenophobia. To these the Eisenhower administration had offered verbal assurances but little political aid. On the other hand, Eisenhower's southern racist supporters had been alienated by the Little Rock episode. On the economic front, the Eisenhower administration had failed to stem the tide of inflation. More important, two severe recessions had occurred, one prior to the 1958 Congressional election and the other as the 1960 presidential wars began.

In foreign policy, the Eisenhower Administration had advanced a less vigorous version of Truman's policy of containment. Talk of "massive retaliation" had become meaningless in the face of the Soviet Union's missile potential. The panacea of "personal diplomacy" had simply been a dangerous illusion which obscured but did not engage the pressing problems of our time. This much could be said: Eisenhower had avoided war. But armed strife in Cuba, Laos, and the Congo led many Americans to wonder how much longer peace could be maintained by timidity. Inevitably, a perplexing question presented itself to tortured advocates of "limited" executive power: could a President be weak at home and yet strong abroad?

To allay the fears inherent in his dilemma, the Republicans offered their adherents a strong man in 1960. He was Richard Milhouse Nixon, twice Vice-President of the United States, and perhaps the most controversial politician of his day. Inevitably associated with the Eisenhower record, Nixon had, nonetheless, differed sharply with the President on some issues. Among these was the issue of "modern Republicanism." Nixon had resented Eisenhower's semantic efforts to recast the party in the image of modern Republicanism. The Vice-President felt that such verbiage unnecessarily alienated the faithful Old Guarders.

Always close to the party machinery, Nixon appreciated and needed Old Guard support as Eisenhower never had. But Nixon was too shrewd to rely entirely on it. He realized that since 1940 the progressives had dominated the Republican presidential nominations. So in a display of consummate political finesse, Nixon managed to convince the eastern and urban wing that he possessed "liberal" and "internationalist" attitudes. The importance of such cautionary consideration became apparent in 1960. As the year began, Nelson Rockefeller, governor of New York, arose to challenge Nixon's hegemony over Republican presidential aspirations. Rockefeller's victory over Averill Harrimann, along with the victory of a young modern Republican, Mark Hatfield, in Oregon, had been two of the few pleasant surprises the Republicans received in 1958. An outspoken liberal, Rockefeller had obvious appeal to Republican progressives. He called for an increased tempo of Republican "modernization." Many conjectured that Rockefeller's proposed "new look" might include himself as a presidential nominee.

But Nixon had built well. The deep-rooted organizational support he had nurtured so carefully held firm through the Rockefeller storm. Reduced to zephyr-like proportions, Rockefeller brought his liberal admonitions to the conference table. He and Nixon met in a New York hotel to seek agreement on party policy. As it happened their joint communique was presented to the Chicago Convention in a package which also contained a presidential candidate. The statement reflected a preponderance of Rockefeller's thinking. For instance, it made much of the "free world confederation." As they had done to many previous internationalist phrases, the Old Guard on the platform committee sheared off this poignant phrase. The issue was not contested. It was looked upon as a necessary concession to the isolationist wing, who were angry at Nixon's insistence on Henry Cabot Lodge as his running mate. Even after the committee's paring, the 1960 platform resolutions were the most liberal that the party has produced. In fact, in marked contrast to the situation of Willkie, Dewey, and Eisenhower, Nixon's record seemed considerably less liberal than his party's platform.

As a Senator, Nixon had supported Taft's economic policies. Nixon has stated, "I oppose the concept of federal involvement whenever it is reasonably possible to find other solutions." On the Communist issue Nixon was anathema to the liberals. When McCarthy was flailing about in 1950 in a frantic attempt to substantiate his fantastic charges of communism in government, Nixon provided him with "names." On the whole, Nixon's "modernistic" inclinations appeared to arise from expedential considerations. In 1959 he told the Young Republicans that "we can't allow the Democrats a monopoly on being for what the people want."

Nixon's foe in 1960 was a man who had risen meteorically to national prominence. Senator John F. Kennedy was defying one of the most stubborn American political prohibitions by his candidacy: the maxim that a Catholic could not become president. In this election a skilled observer might have questioned the validity of the anti-Catholic prohibition on purely pragmatic grounds. For many of Eisenhower's neo-isolationist supporters were Catholic, and probably susceptible to a *pro*-Catholic appeal. In addition it would be widely assumed that Kennedy, as an Irish Catholic, was congenitally anti-Communist. His pointed absence during the McCarthy censure would enhance his stature with the "disillusionists."

Nixon could not afford to lose such sizable blocs of Eisenhower supporters, but he did. Thus, by a narrow margin, John Fitgzerald Kennedy was elected President of the United States on November 6, 1960. In retrospect, the 1960 campaign seems unusually devoid of issues. Such devices as the series of television debates emphasized the personalities of the candidates to an unprecedented degree. The issues were there, they simply were not discussed. One is struck by such factors as the interminable length of time that Nixon spent haggling over the insignificant islands of Quemoy and Matsu while utterly ignoring the broader consideration of Far Eastern policy.

Upon careful scrutiny, Kennedy's "New Frontier" resembles nothing so much as the New Deal warmed over. But it was sufficient, since the Republicans offered no effective alternatives.

Shoemaker in the Chicago American

"Did you hear something, Rocky?"

Vicky in the London New Statesman

THE REPUBLICAN DILEMMA

It is tempting to conclude this analysis with certain analogies between the present and the past. For instance, it might be interesting to compare the approaches of Governor George Romney and Wendell Willkie. Romney's talk of the citizen in politics, and Willkie's "We, The People" approach seem to have a great deal in common. Willkie's distaste for "bigness" in any segment of American life is echoed in the Michigan Governor's dislike for the contemporary corporate and business structure in this country. Romney also appears to have the ability to sell himself whether he is out beating the hustings for Rambler or attempting to entice business into Michigan. As a big businessman who is an opponent of economic exploitation, Romney shares an attribute which Willkie used to good advantage in 1940. Comparisons of this type could go on to the point of proclaiming that with slight variations Romney is a latter-day Wendell Willkie. But such comparisons add little to the understanding of the dilemma which confronts the Republican party. They merely indicate that the party has an unorthodox personality of sufficient national prominence to warrant consideration as a presidential candidate.

It also might be interesting to speculate on the delegate strength which Goldwater, Rockefeller, and the favorite sons will possess at the 1964 convention. There also is the fascinating comparison between the late Senator Taft and Senator Goldwater. An attempt to explain why Goldwater's Gallup poll standing is better than Taft's was, could prove to be an excellent study in political personalities. But to do this would be to miss the great conflict which grips the Republican party.

Certain observers — and indeed Senator Goldwater himself — maintain that Rockefeller and Arizona's junior senator are not very far apart on basic issues. A careful review of their public statements indicates that, although there are areas of difference between the two, their stand on issues has been getting closer. This would appear to be a normal process in their efforts to secure the Republican presidential nomination in 1964. More important, it signifies the continuing dichotomy between the party's progressive and conservative wings.

Before proceeding with an analysis of the dilemma which faces the Republican party, it should be made clear that there is a possibility that neither Rockefeller nor Goldwater will receive the Republican presidential nomination in either 1964 or 1968. There are other eligible contenders such as Governors Romney, Scranton and Hatfield. Among members of Congress, men like Senator Thurston Morton and Representatives Gerald Ford of Michigan and John Lindsay of New York could under certain circumstances become candidates. Of course, the party might turn to a military hero such as one of the generals, Lucius Clay or Lauris Norstad. If the party followed this course, it would be operating within a successful historical pattern. In 1840, the Whigs were able to break the Democratic hold on the office with General Harrison. The Republicans turned to General Grant in 1868 to keep their party together and to insure their continued control of the presidency. And in 1952, the nomination of General Eisenhower was motivated, at least in part, by the desire to win and at the same time to solidify the party and obscure the fundamental differences over matters of policy.

The Republicans might turn to one of these other men or to an outright dark horse, but the candidacies of Rockefeller and Goldwater have created the greatest interest. These two men, although softening their stand on some issues in order to be less objectionable to each other's potential supporters, represent the dilemma which the Republicans have faced since 1940. As an eastern seaboard liberal who has not hesitated to agree with and to serve Democratic presidents when he believed it was the right thing to do, Rockefeller is the heir apparent to the Republican party's progressive wing. Barry Goldwater is the obvious favorite of the conservatives. This wing of the party is so enamored of the Senator that they have discarded the label of "Taft Republicans" and have become "Goldwater Republicans." Goldwater's books, *The Conscience of a Conservative* and *Why Not Victory?'* have become their political bibles.

Goldwater offers the conservatives the first completely acceptable candidate they have had in over a decade. As I have pointed out, the conservatives have not been able to nominate a candidate of their choosing in the past six national conventions. Through this period the conservatives have grumbled and briefly rebelled against the liberal control of the conventions. Despite its convention failures, however, the Taft-

Goldwater wing of the party has held many of the important party offices during the past twenty-four years. And the Republican liberals like Senators Javits, Case, and Cooper have never constituted more than a vocal minority of the party's congressional delegation.

The fact that Republican conservatives have controlled many party and congressional leadership posts is not difficult to understand. In the first place, the traditional areas of Republican strength tend to be in the rural areas of the Midwest. It was here that the party's electoral revival occurred after the Democratic onslaughts of 1932, 1934, and 1936. Men like Dirksen, Halleck, Taft, and Mundt got to Congress at least ten years before the liberal Republicans from the east and west coasts were able to capture congressional seats. During these years, the conservatives gained party and legislative seniority.

It is also important in understanding the prominence of the congressional Republicans to recall that they have developed political friendships with conservative southern Democrats. This alliance not only worked to the detriment of the national Democratic party, but it also strengthened the hand of the conservatives in the Republican party. Moreover, the union of southern Democrats and conservative Republicans makes it appear that the Republicans are calling many of the shots in Congress. Republican conservatives have possessed legislative power, particularly to halt legislation, far in excess of their numbers. The voting alliance of southern Democrats has been politically profitable for the Republican conservatives in and out of Congress. They can point out that President Kennedy cannot get his program through Congress because a large number of Democrats refuse to support it.

During the Republican party's period in the political wilderness, the congressional conservatives have had a public platform from which to express their views. Few Republican liberals, on the other hand, possess this ready made forum. They have to be content with making their voices heard through some state governors, a few Republican senators, and during presidential election years. Moreover, those who support the Republican liberals are not professional politicians to the same extent as their conservative counterparts. The amateurism fostered by Wendell Willkie has been a lasting attribute of the Republican progressives. These amateurs are the "citizen type." They do not possess the single-minded dedication to politics of the conservatives. The amateurs are the country-club set who express their civic urge through a variety of activities. They can be found leading the community chest drive, serving on civic improvement committees, working with the Red Cross, and supporting that which they consider to be worthwhile. Such activity does not leave sufficient time to perform the day-to-day, dull work which is required to keep a party organization together. By-and-large, many of these people consider politics a dirty business. They are attracted to the reform candidates who give promise of breaking the professionals' control over the party.

Contrasted with the amateur who appears at election or convention time is the party regular. For the most part, the regulars tend to be conservative. They have no illusions about the possibilities of reforming mankind overnight. Since they know many of the community secrets, they do not particularly conceive of their activities being out of keeping with social mores. They do participate in community affairs, but their participation is usually an adjunct to their party activity. The faithful workers accept these responsibilities to maintain a degree of public respectability and to keep open the channels of communication with various elements in the community.

The regulars generally have given long service to their party. During their years of service, they have developed respect for the conservative members of their party who have managed to hold on to their congressional seats. When they gather for Lincoln Day dinners, they frequently hear speeches for the party's congressional wing. Year after year they have heard cries of indignation over the sky-rocketing national debt, expanding public welfare programs, and the drift towards socialism. Yet, when presidential nominating time rolls around, the regulars hear from their liberal colleagues who are eager to undo the work of the preceding three years. Every four years the party faithful nourish the hope that this time one of their own kind will get the party's highest reward. In each convention beginning with 1940, the regulars have been disappointed. Good party members that they are, they swallow their feelings and go to work for a man who is not one of them. For six months they put up with the amateurs and their citizens' committees for Willkie or Eisenhower. The regulars even become enthusiastic about the presidential candidate and forget that they had vowed to quit the party if their man was not nominated.

It is not easy for the regulars to do this, but they do it for a combination of reasons. They have been told that a conservative just cannot win the urban states and without these states the presidency can never be gained. To the conservative party worker, who is after all a realist, this seems to be the case. When they look over the list of state electoral college votes they can see that it is almost impossible to win without carrying a majority of the big states. They may wonder how Taft or Dirksen even made it to the Senate from an urban state, but they are told that their man may be popular in his home state but that this popularity does not penetrate the entire complex of urban states.

The party faithful also know that their amateur friends will quickly disappear once the election is over. The few who do remain will probably be integrated into the existing organization and become regulars. Even if a liberal should be elected, the regulars will reassert control over the party. Indeed, the regulars feel that they may be able to ride the liberal coattails to power. The regulars also know that regardless of who occupies the White House their kind will have the most important voices in Congress.

Much more could be said about the conservatives' willingness to remain in and work for the Republican party. It probably can be summed up by saying that the nature of the federal system and separation of powers makes it possible for their voices to be heard and their influence to be felt. So long as they can hold on, conservatives have hope that one day a candidate of their choosing will be nominated and elected. This hope plus their congressional friends sustains the conservative wing of the Republican party.

In some ways the Republican liberals are in a more advantageous position than the Old Guard. The progressives do not have the same personal stake in party affairs. When it counts — at the national conventions — they have been able to cart off the prize. Unlike the conservatives, they are not in fundamental disagreement with the policies of a Democratic president. To the liberals and their amateur supporters, the party organization is important only if it can be used periodically to put one of their candidates over. The progressives are not particularly happy with the foot-dragging practices of Republican congressional leaders. However, the party legislative members and their supporters have generally helped the progressive candidates, rather than sit on their hands or defect to the Democrats. In short, the progressives know that the conservatives, unless they are southerners, do not have a political home outside the Republican party.

Any picture of Republican conservatives and liberals is likely to be a generalization which does not cover all the relationships that exist between them. Both groups are motivated by the primary political goal of gaining and retaining public office. This cannot be achieved without a great deal of compromise and collaboration among party members of all shades of opinion. The liberals are not as "starry-eyed" in these matters as they have been pictured. And the conservatives are not as hardened as they may appear. Republican progressives and conservatives alike have been willing to recognize that politics is the art of the possible. Both groups can become genuinely enthusiastic about a candidate who is not of their persuasion. In other words, as Republicans they have accepted the "rules of the game" which go along with active party membership. The most fundamental of these rules is that regardless of the candidates selected to represent the party in an electoral contest, party members will support them.

Despite the active cooperation in the past between Republican conservatives and progressives, there is every indication that the party may be headed for a decade of battles which could make the 1940 and 1952 conventions look like church picnics. The primary reason for this is that the conservatives no longer appear to be content to accept the notion that one of their own must take a back seat to a progressive. The immense popular appeal of Goldwater has provided the regulars with a candidate who seems to have the support of Democrats, particularly those in the South.

Party conservatives argue that the solid South can be permanently shattered with a conservative Republican presidential nominee. This prospect has a great deal of appeal to Republican professionals for at least two reasons. First, if a conservative could carry the South and the traditional areas of Republican strength in the Midwest and Rocky Mountain states, it would not be imperative to carry a majority of the large urban states to win. Professionals feel that a Goldwater just might be able to do this. Thus, with the scent of victory in their nostrils, the progressive arguments no longer make the same impression on the conservatives. The objective of nominating a candidate who can carry the industrial states of the eastern seaboard no longer seems too important. Although delegates to future Republican conventions will continue to make compromises and concessions, visions of electoral success in the South have made the conservatives determined to see that it is the progressives who give in.

The complete dismantling of the solid Democratic south with a conservative nominee has a second appeal for Republican professionals. Republicans have not written off congressional seats in the large states, but they realize that every gain made in them will require much effort and money. The South, in the light of certain limited Republican success during the past decade, appears to be ripe for plucking. A conservative at the top of the ticket would encourage Republicans to file for state and national offices in the south. Undoubtedly, most of these office seekers would align themselves with the party's presidential nominee. In such circumstances and in view of the apparent hostility of many southerners to the national Democratic party, a conservative Republican presidential nominee could pull many Republican representatives and senators into office. To many Republicans this prospect is so alluring that they contend it would be worth nominating a conservative even if he lost the election for chief executive.

The growing Republican strength in the South, which could be turned into a stampede to the party with the "right" candidate at the head of the ticket, is a development which many progressives view as a mixed blessing. Greater Republican congressional representation from the South would tend to place the progressives in more of a minority. If southern Republicans were segregationist — and there is every reason to believe that this would be the case — as well as conservative, the liberals would have an even more difficult time shaping national party pronouncements designed to appeal to minority groups. No longer could liberal Republicans point to the Democratic party as composed of factions which support mutually exclusive positions on the race issue. Currently, Republicans are somewhat divided on the race issues, but their divisions are not nearly so deep as those within the Democratic party. Moreover, the Democratic party has learned to live with this situation even though it is extremely uncomfortable. Republican progressives have no desire to inherit what is probably the most serious problem within the Democratic party.

Most conservative Republicans who support civil rights do not share the misgivings of their progressive colleagues. Additional Republican congressmen from the South should mean that the position of the present conservative leaders would be enhanced. With a larger number of conservative Republicans in the national legislature, a future Republican president or aspirant for the office would have to pay more attention to the congressional party.

The upshot of all this is that the party conservatives will be bolder in making their wishes felt in a national convention. However, the likelihood that the conservatives will demand a candidate of their own choosing is not dependent either upon projected electoral successes in the South or upon the fact that the conservatives believe they have a potential presidential winner in Barry Goldwater. As important as these two factors appear to be, there is a deeper reason for their resurgence. For over two decades the conservatives have bought the progressive reasoning that only a liberal can win the presidency. During these years the party has had only one successful presidential candidate. Many conservatives argue that Eisenhower was not elected because he was sponsored by the party's progressive wing, but because he was the greatest national folk-hero since Franklin Roosevelt. Following this line of reasoning, conservatives argue that for all of its modern Republicanism, the party is in little better shape than it was two decades ago. They contend that it is time to stop experimenting with new Republicanism and reassert the traditional party policies.

The party regulars have been reinforced by various organizations in the battle against the "me too" type Republicanism. Beginning in the late 1950's, a number of conservative and right-wing groups began to appear on the political scene. The strongest of these is the John Birch Society (JBS) which seems to have latched on to conservative Republican candidates throughout the country. In many cases JBS members and others of their ilk were not active in politics prior to their affiliation with the anti-communist and anti-socialist crusades. In this regard they have a certain similarity to the amateurs who are the mainstay of the Republican progressives in that neither groups consider political party membership as the most important aspect of civic activity. Following the instructions of Robert Welch and ex-Congressman John Rousselot of California, JBS members have infiltrated the Republican party, particularly in the western states.

Right-wing conservatism seems to have a great appeal for young people as is evidenced by the spread of Young Americans for Freedom (YAF) chapters to many American college campuses. The 1963 national Young Republican convention gave every indication of being dominated by conservatives, many of whom appear to be members of or in sympathy with the JBS and YAF. The rising tide of conservatism among young people and the growth of right-wing organizations such as the JBS should be of assistance to the party regulars, but it also creates very serious problems for them. There is evidence that the militant conservatives of the "far right" plan an eventual take-over of the Republican party machinery. Robert Welch suggests this course of action in *The Blue Book* which is the founding document of the JBS.

There are many who think the power of the new right-wing organizations has been greatly exaggerated. The defeat of the three JBS Congressmen from California in 1962 plus the favorable response to Republican denunciations of the radical right are said to be indicators of the general public rejection of extremist groups. Correct as this may be, there are also indications that the conservative Republican resurgence stems in part from the efforts of the JBS and YAF. Certainly, these groups with a single-minded determination will fight for the nomination and election of conservatives at all levels of government. In this situation the long-time party conservatives will have to engage in conflict with both the progressives and the upstarts on the right. If the party regulars actively collaborate with the extremists in securing the nomination of Senator Goldwater, there is every possibility that the voters will deal the Republican party a solid defeat.

A final factor which should be mentioned in connection with the conservative revival is that many of the leaders are getting old. Men like Dirksen, Halleck, and Mundt must realize that if they are going to be on the scene when one of their breed leads the country, it will have to be within the next decade. The loyalty and devotion of these men and their colleagues to the Republican party has been of the highest order. They have spoken and traveled wherever the faithful asked them in their quest for whatever votes were to be had. Although they must realize that the party would not accept anyone of them as a nominee, the party at least owes them a candidate to whom they can give their wholehearted support. This does not mean that all three — Dirksen, Halleck and Mundt — will back the same man. It does mean that all three are apt to insist on a thoroughly regular Republican.

To this point it might seem that the party is on the verge of rejecting all it appeared to embrace since Willkie's nomination. The Republican party, if it is to remain a major party, cannot retreat to the blissful era of normalcy. Nor can it present either a united progressive or conservative front to the voters. In all probability, however, the party will unite around a personality in hopes of regaining the presidency. This will be the case whether the candidate leans in the direction of conservatism or progressivism. And future Republican nominees are apt to *lean* toward one of these positions, although their most ardent supporters may claim them as thorough-going conservatives or progressives.

The conclusion to be drawn is that the major wings of the party, despite the fact that their strength has a different base, are of about equal importance. Any man who desires the party's nomination has to do more than convince one wing of the party he should have it. A one-sided appeal would have the effect of alienating a sizable bloc of Republican party workers as well as voters of both parties. The notion that future Republican nominees will tend toward the middle-of-the-road is based on the premise that the professionals and candidates will want to win.

Either the progressives or conservatives could become gripped with a "death wish" for their party. In fact, a small minority of both wings probably do not care whether the Republican party continues to exist. Some conservatives have openly suggested a third party movement which would unite southern Democrats and conservative Republicans.

Some liberals have privately admitted that their sentiments are already expressed by the national Democratic party. The most serious progressive defection from the Republican party was Senator Wayne Morse. Although there are signs that a few Republicans would destroy their party, the past history of the party indicates that this probably will not grow to serious proportions.

Despite the probability that upcoming Republican national conventions will select moderates, does not the future look dark for the progressives? If Goldwater or someone with similar basic support is nominated, regardless of the extent to which he moderates his position on issues, would it not mean the ascendency of the conservatives? The answer to these questions lie in the preceding chapters. If as I have observed in this chapter, the party conservatives are not dying out or even fading away, it is equally correct that the party progressives are not on the verge of extinction. Indeed, the progressive wing of the party has an articulate group of spokesmen who possess the glamour to stir the hearts of the party and the voters.

More significant than the personalities of either wing is the fact that the situation is not conducive to a renunciation of the basic principles for which Willkie stood. For more than twenty years a majority of the Republican party has accepted the social and economic reforms of the New Deal. The party platforms have contained promises to enlarge some of these programs while suggesting changes in others. In foreign affairs, the party has supported the UN, regional treaty alliances such as NATO, and foreign military and economic assistance.

Not only has the Republican party accepted these domestic and international policies, but the majority of the American people through their ballots and through the polled indication of their preferences support such programs. In the face of the Republican party's continued support and the backing of voters of both parties, it is highly unlikely that, as long as the domestic and foreign situations remain basically unchanged, there will be a fundamental shift in national and international policy. All of this could change if there was a severe crisis at home or abroad. If this did occur, the whole country and not just the Republican party would be affected.

The responsiveness of the Republican party to changing conditions accounts for its acceptance of the progressive wing. However, all members have not been willing to make a conversion to this position, just as there are Democrats who have been unwilling to accept the domestic reforms and international policies of the past three decades. Although the dilemma which confronts the Republican party has been the concern of this book, it is in reality a problem of broader proportions. In fact, it is woven in the fabric of American politics. It is more serious for the Republicans because of two factors.

First, the Republicans were turned out of power in 1932 when they could not come up with an immediate solution to the problems created by the Great Depression. The policies adopted in response to this situation were not of Republican origin. Most Republicans were so shocked by the Depression that they either accepted the Roosevelt reforms or blindly criticized them. It was not until 1938 that the party began to think in terms of alternatives to the New Deal. Shortly after 1938, the whole country became preoccupied with international events. Hence, the party has spent the best part of three decades involved in an internal dispute over programs which did not originate with the Republicans.

A second factor which has caused splits within the Republican ranks is America's involvement in world politics. The Republicans were out of power during World War II and the first seven years of the post-war period. They did not have direct access to the most important centers — Presidency, Department of State, and the agencies responsible for military affairs — for making and implementing international policy. Just as had been the case in the early 1930's, the Republicans could only react against or cooperate with the Administration. There was considerable Republican support for the war and post-war policies of Roosevelt and Truman, as reflected in the concept of a bi-partisan foreign policy. When the Republicans came to power in 1952, there was little that could be done or little apparent desire to alter substantially the policies set into motion by the two preceding Administrations. The chronic post-war crisis and the inability of either Democratic or Republican presidents to change the situation has created a great deal of frustration within the conservative wing of the G.O.P. Undoubtedly, the foreign situation has stimulated the growth of the right wing.

In effect, the Republicans' dilemma is not of their own making, but this does not lessen the problems which it presents. The party's progressives have little more to offer than a promise to administer better the foreign and domestic programs which have their origins in Democratic administrations. The conservatives, on the other hand, seem to fall into two general types. There are those like Senator John Tower of Texas who resist most attempts to expand the activities of the national government. Moreover, he advocates a reduction and in some cases a complete withdrawal of federal governmental activity in favor of state programs. There are many conservatives who do not even bother to offer specific programs. In the words of William Buckley, editor of *The National Review,* this group contends that they "will not willingly cede more power to anyone, not to the state, not to General Motors, not to the CIO." This, Buckley concedes, is a "No-Program."

There is more that could be said by way of elaborating the dilemma which faces the Republican party. These roads of analysis lead back to the same basic conclusion — the Republican party is a mirror of the problems with which Americans have wrestled since 1930. It is the G.O.P., as the party held responsible for the depression of the 1930's, which has been trying to devise a formula which will return them to power. Divisions within the party have been magnified out of proportion, because Republicans have not possessed the prerequisites which accompany control of the national government. In other words, the Democrats through their domination of national offices have been able to smooth over many problems within their party. For over three decades the foreign and domestic programs of F.D.R., with but slight alterations, have been the basis of the Democratic appeal to the electorate. The Republicans have not been able to match the attraction of this program.

The majority of Republicans have accepted the idea that there can be no return to the "good old days" when they considered themselves the only party fit to govern. However, they have not been able to offer the voters an alternative to the "New Deal," "Fair Deal," and "New Frontier." National liberal leaders have been accepted, because nothing better was offered by the conservatives. However, the progressive attitude of Republican presidential candidates has never been adopted by a large segment of the party organization. Beginning with Willkie's nomination, the liberals have had to rely on the fears of the party regulars and conservatives to gain the presidential nomination. Some progressives would argue that the party will have to have another Willkie before they can control the party. This is naïve in view of the problems which confront the party.

The only conclusion which can be supported by study of the past and present situations is that the Republican dilemma will continue into the foreseeable future. Such a conclusion will not give comfort to either the progressives or conservatives. It is one of the realities of American politics.

Fitzpatrick in the St. Louis Post-Dispatch

Road To November

INDEX

The index for this book was prepared by Louis D. Hayes, a graduate student in the Department of Government at the University of Arizona.

100

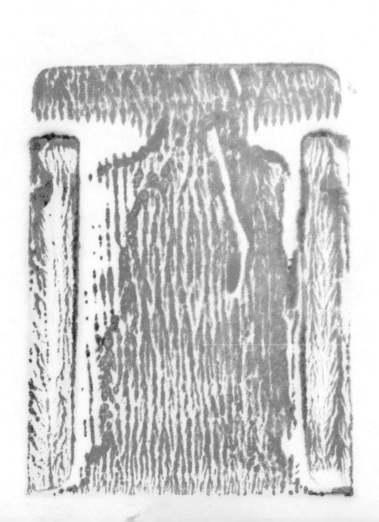